A Writer's Craft

Kendall Dunkelberg

A Writer's Craft

Multi-Genre Creative Writing

macmillan education palgrave

First published 2017 by
PALGRAVE

Palgrave in the UK is an imprint of Macmillan Publishers Limited, registered in England, company number 785998, of 4 Crinan Street, London, N1 9XW.

Palgrave® and Macmillan® are registered trademarks in the United States, the United Kingdom, Europe and other countries.

ISBN 978–1–137–61095–9 hardback
ISBN 978–1–137–61094–2 paperback

This book is printed on paper suitable for recycling and made from fully managed and sustained forest sources. Logging, pulping and manufacturing processes are expected to conform to the environmental regulations of the country of origin.

A catalogue record for this book is available from the British Library.

A catalog record for this book is available from the Library of Congress.

Contents

Acknowledgments

I am very grateful to all my students in creative writing at Mississippi University for Women over the past 20 years and more. I have learned more from working with you than you could ever realize. I am proud of your accomplishments and grateful that I have had the opportunity to share in your writing. I am also deeply indebted to the great writers and teachers I have known over the years, especially Sam Moon and Robin Metz at Knox College, Marc Kelly Smith, Cin Salach, and Sheila Donohue of the poetry slams at the Green Mill and David Hernandez of Street Sounds and the Urban Studies program in Chicago, as well as André Lefevere at the University of Texas at Austin. I have also learned much from Carol Burke, Molly Best Tinsley, Heather Sellers, and Janet Burroway, whose textbooks I used before deciding to develop *A Writer's Craft*. The Creative Writing Pedagogy group on Facebook has been a valuable source of ideas and resources both for this book and for my teaching.

Many thanks to Stephanie Vanderslice and Dana Chamblee Carpenter who read early drafts of this book and gave insightful criticism and encouragement, to Anna Leahy and Mary Cantrell for their encouragement and the many conversations we've had about writing over the years, and to Graeme Harper who read the manuscript and helped me find a home for it at Palgrave. I am extremely grateful to my editor, Rachel Bridgewater, and her creative team for their attention to detail and for the beautiful cover and design of this book. I am also thankful for my colleagues at Mississippi University for Women, especially my department chair, Bridget Smith Pieschel; dean, Brian Anderson; provost, Tom Richardson; and president, Jim Borsig, who have supported me and the creative writing program over the years.

Finally, special thanks to my wife, Kim Whitehead, and son, Aidan, without whose support this book would not be possible. Our many conversations about teaching, writing, life, and art, as well as your patience and understanding as I have taken on this and other projects have kept me going and provided inspiration.

About the Author

Kendall Dunkelberg is Director of Creative Writing at Mississippi University for Women where he heads the low-residency MFA program, the undergraduate concentration, and the minor in creative writing. He directs the Eudora Welty Writers' Symposium, is a past president and co-executive director of the Southern Literary Festival Association, and has taught a multi-genre introduction to creative writing for over 20 years. He has been awarded a Mellon Fellowship to the University of Texas at Austin and two Fulbright Fellowships to conduct dissertation research at the University of Ghent and to teach at the Catholic University in Leuven, Belgium. He is also a recipient of a Mississippi Arts Commission Artist Fellowship for his poetry.

Dunkelberg has published three collections of poetry, *Barrier Island Suite: Poems Inspired by the Life and Art of Walter Inglis Anderson*, *Time Capsules*, and *Landscapes and Architectures*, as well as a collection of translated poems by the Flemish poet Paul Snoek, *Hercules, Richelieu, and Nostradamus*. He guest-edited and translated poetry and fiction for *Outside the Lines: New Dutch and Flemish Writing*, a special issue of *The Literary Review*, and his poems and translations have appeared in many other magazines and in *The Southern Poetry Anthology, Volume 2: Mississippi* and *Down to the Dark River: Contemporary Poems about the Mississippi River*. He also serves as faculty advisor to *The Dilettanti*, the undergraduate literary magazine at Mississippi University for Women, and as editor of *Poetry South* and advisor to *Ponder Review*, published by the graduate program.

1

Introduction

What Is Creative Writing?

This is probably the first question you have. Or maybe you already think you know the answer, since you signed up to take a course called Creative Writing or something similar. In all likelihood, you do have some good ideas about what creative writing is, but you may also wonder what distinguishes it from other kinds of writing. The easy answer is that creative writing includes drama, fiction, nonfiction, and poetry. Those are the main forms of writing that we will look at in this textbook. The answer becomes a little harder when we try to define what makes these forms different from other forms of writing, so here's another way to look at it.

In most of your other classes, you probably write essays. One might argue that the essay is one form and creative writing uses other forms. Yet when we discuss nonfiction, we will talk about the essay as one form that you might use in creative writing (and we will even talk about the differences between nonfiction and creative nonfiction). So there is a gray area between what we might classify as creative writing and other forms. Perhaps the best way to think about the difference is by looking at the kind of assignments that are given in creative writing versus other classes. In a literature class, you might be asked to analyze a piece of literature and give your interpretation. Or in a history class, you might be asked to discuss the causes or the effects of an event. You have a specific topic that defines your task, and you write about it, using evidence to support the assertions you want to make. We sometimes call this expository writing because you, the writer, are exploring or explaining something else. The main inspiration for the writing seems to come from the subject you are writing about.

In a creative writing class, though, the assignment is more likely to be to write a poem, write a scene for a story, or eventually write the whole story from beginning to end. An assignment may give you more guidelines than that (e.g. to write about a specific subject or to write using a specific form), but even then, much of what you write has to come from yourself. You create the topic rather than explore a topic that already exists. Your subjective experience of that topic, your emotional response or your inner contemplation becomes a major part of your writing, much more so than if you were writing up a lab report or case study.

Of course, this is a somewhat arbitrary distinction that doesn't always hold true, and I feel a little ambiguous about presenting it as a definition. Many textbooks do, and it may be a useful distinction. The truth is, though, that all writing can be creative, and the forms we call creative writing can include elements of expository writing. Creative writing can be very objective at times and may concentrate more on finding beauty in language than in expressing emotion, for instance. Expository writing, for all its attempts at objectivity, has been shown to have a subjective component—subjectivity is nearly impossible to avoid entirely. And a lab report may be beautifully written as well as informative. So the difference is largely one of degree and perhaps of intent: expository writing makes more of an attempt to be objective compared to the stated goal in creative writing of being subjective.

But in terms of thinking about what you will do in an introductory creative writing class, this may be a useful place to start, since most of the ideas that you decide to work on will come from your own imagination. You may get at them from many different sources, but ultimately, you will make them your own. This can be a little daunting, especially for students who are used to working on more traditional assignments. You've gotten good at expository writing, and for some students it can be a challenge to approach a new kind of assignment that seems to have no rules and no limits. However, there is a long history of teaching creative writing in an academic setting, and the way a course like this is structured will help you reach the ultimate goal of a finished portfolio of your own creative writing.

How Is Creative Writing Taught?

In this book, we will use a number of strategies common to creative writing as an academic discipline. In the early chapters, I encourage you to do a lot of writing and to try exercises in your writing journal to get you started and to give you something to work on in a group. You may want to choose which of those you want to develop into finished products, and you may be able to focus on other stories, poems, essays, or scripts that don't start out as an exercise. Yet starting out based on an exercise or prompt can help you get to ideas that you wouldn't think of on your own. The exercise itself may not supply the idea, but focusing on the demands of the prompt allows you to get started writing and lets your mind supply the content.

One of the main emphases of many creative writing classes is collaborative writing and group work. Often in the early stages of writing, we will work together to develop ideas or to begin shaping the exercises you have started in your journal. As we work together to develop ideas, we will also work on developing a good group dynamic. This is important to foster communication needed to discuss each other's work in writing workshops. You will develop the trust and the skills to give your peers good advice. But don't worry that you have to have the "right" answers or advice. Your honest opinion about what you have read is the most helpful advice you can give your peers. You don't have to tell them how to "fix" what they have written; just tell them what you got out of it. It will be their responsibility to decide how to adjust so that most readers have the response they want. And they may even be surprised to learn that people got more out of their writing than they intended.

I often suggest starting with exercises in small groups, then moving toward more formal workshops in small groups with early drafts that are based on exercises everyone has done, and working toward more formal workshops later, when everyone discusses the nearly finished work each writer has chosen to bring to workshop. Another model is to begin with formal workshops much sooner, and a third method is to avoid the workshop model entirely and focus on working in smaller groups.

Along with exercises and workshops, we will study many of the forms and literary terms associated with creative writing. These terms will help you discuss your writing with others, and they should prove useful in discussing literature or if you ever find yourself teaching writing or language arts. We will also begin the discussion of the process of literary citizenship and publishing in the appendix.

The main work that you do in a creative writing class, though, will likely be developing a portfolio of your creative writing. Once you have an idea, which may come from an exercise or may come from your own writing, you will develop it into a finished poem, story, essay, or script. Group sessions or workshops will help you reach this point, as will individual conferences, if those are available.

The Writer as Reader

Writers need to know what other writers are doing. We are all inspired, not only by writers of the past, but also by writers of today. We want to remain current, and we want our writing to fit in with current trends or to buck those trends, but how will we know that we are working with or against the grain if we don't read in the grain? To learn what other writers are writing, you will want to begin reading literary magazines, current anthologies, or other outlets for contemporary writing in your region, your country, or the world.

When writers read, we look at a text differently than literary scholars do. Actually, many writers are also literary scholars, so they may do both kinds of reading, but when thinking about what they read as a writer, they look for different things. First and foremost, writers read for enjoyment. We don't necessarily analyze everything we read. We don't necessarily try to form an interpretation, though sometimes we can't help ourselves.

Instead, when writers read, we often look at *how* a poem, story, essay, or play is written, and not only at *what* it is trying to say. We read to see how it's done, not to copy exactly, but to learn from other writers and to adapt what they do to our own work. Copying exactly what another writer has written would be plagiarism, of course. But even being too heavily influenced by another writer can lead to writing that is uninteresting. Whenever a writer "steals" from another writer (as some like to call it), she or he does try to make it her or his own. Yet most writers acknowledge the influence of others, especially early in their career. You can emulate another writer without copying their style exactly. So as you read, think about how a story or poem is put together and consider the choices you might make. You might try to write in a similar vein, or you might try to write in contrast to the work you have read. In either case, there is some influence, yet you also strike out on your own.

How Is This Book Organized?

As you might have guessed by now, I do not expect you to know much yet about the forms, or *genres*, that we will study. In the first chapters, we will concentrate on getting started writing and on issues that are common to all genres: drama, fiction, nonfiction, and poetry. In fact, for your earliest drafts, you may not even know what genre you want to work in. Exercises may ask you to write lists or to start with a prose paragraph. Then you may work on the different forms this might take. In later chapters, we will begin to study some of the conventions of these four genres. By this point, you will likely have decided which of your texts will be poems, essays, stories, or scripts, though as they develop, you may still change your mind. I have found that it is usually better, especially for writers in the early stages of their careers, not to decide too early what form they want to work in. I encourage everyone to try all four genres, though you may eventually decide which ones you want to focus on. But to decide what form a text will take too early in the process can limit how you develop the idea, and that can cause problems. If you remain open to many possibilities of form, you may be surprised at the way the writing turns out. We will discuss why this is the case more in Chapter 2, as we discuss the writing process.

A Note to the Instructor

When I first sat down to write the notes that became this textbook, I was of two minds: on the one hand, I have always enjoyed using someone else's textbook for the opportunity it provided at times to argue with another author; on the other hand, after teaching creative writing for 20 years, I felt I had something to say that was lacking in the books I had used. My biggest concern was that if I wrote my own textbook, I wouldn't be able to argue with myself. There are many ways to teach creative writing and many approaches to fiction, poetry, nonfiction, and drama. I don't claim to have all of the answers. What I have tried to do is to put forward a unified and cohesive approach. At times, I have tried to present a range of views; at other times, the need for cohesion has limited the number of views I can express.

That is where you come in, of course. I encourage you to give your students your own experience, to argue with positions I take, or to try out alternative strategies. I assume that you generally agree with much of what is said in this book or you would likely choose a different one, but I also assume you have your own examples, your own anecdotes, your own way of talking about how to write and how to teach creative writing. You may even decide you would rather rearrange the chapters in this book, and teach them in a different order. I've done that many times with other books, so I could hardly argue with you now.

Though I've written the chapters to build on one another, it may be that for your strengths as a teacher or for your students, you find another order works better. Especially when we get to the chapters on genre, I think they could be taught in any order, though I find that starting with nonfiction is a good choice, and for practical reasons it's easier for students to move to poetry before writing something as long as a story. Drama tends to work well at the end because students are often less familiar. I have even included some material in the appendix because I assume you're likely to make very different choices about if and when to incorporate it, depending on the class, your school's calendar, etc. I also highly recommend assigning an anthology, literary magazine, course packet, or links to online texts in addition to this book to provide recent examples of creative writing.

Because I feel a textbook should be a starting point and not the final say in teaching a subject, on the companion website for this book, we will create a space where you can share ideas for additional resources, exercises, class activities, and pedagogical discussions. Please visit us and join the conversation at www.palgravehighered.com/dunkelberg.

A Note to the Student

If you are like me, you probably just read the note to your instructor, so you will know that I encourage instructors to engage with this book, rearrange it, even argue with it. Writers love to argue about what we do, and sometimes we take very energetic positions. Yet by and large we try to show respect for one another. If your instructor has another way to explain a concept or if she or he uses different terminology, there's nothing wrong with that. It may depend on your culture or on your instructor's background. Or it may be a matter of personal preference.

You should also ask questions and look for your own answers. Be an active learner, in other words, and don't expect the book to have all the answers already. A textbook like this is there to introduce you to the topic, to get you to try new things and to ask questions that you wouldn't have thought to ask. Your answers and your instructor's answers are just as valid as mine, but I hope this book brings the subject of creative writing together in such a way that you move further along on your journey as a writer than you would have on your own.

For those who may be reading this book outside of any class and without an instructor, I encourage you to find a group of other writers to share your thoughts and your writing with. We learn most from the vital conversations we have with other writers and with sympathetic and perceptive readers. A creative writing class is one of the best places to find a community of writers and readers, yet if you don't have the structured environment of a classroom, you can always create a community on your own.

The companion website for the textbook has resources for students as well as instructors, including links to resources for writers, additional writing exercises, a discussion area, etc. Please join us at www. palgravehighered.com/dunkelberg.

2

The Writing Process

Inspiration

A common image of the writer is of someone who is suddenly struck with inspiration, like a bolt of lightning. He or she rushes to the typewriter (or these days to a keyboard, but in the old days to a roll of parchment and a quill pen) and dashes off a few perfect lines. This is the romantic idea of the poet: Wordsworth walking through daffodils, then sitting down later to pen "I Wandered Lonely as a Cloud." It's a nice idea, but it's terribly unrealistic. I'm not saying that poems or even stories never seem to happen this way—some writers do report times when writing seems this inspired, and even I have had some poems that seemed to come to me fully formed. But it can be a debilitating model to try to live up to, and even when the writing does seem to flow from the pen, I would argue that it usually does so, not only because the writer is inspired by the muse, but also because the writer has done many things prior to that experience to cultivate the muse.

Look at it in another way. How often have you been inspired to write in the last year or so? When you did sit down to write, was the initial product perfect? If you're a typical student, my guess is you answered that you wrote a few times in the past year and the writing you produced was less than perfect. Otherwise, why would you sign up for this class or buy this book? If you already write perfectly, then you should quit school, move to Hollywood, New York, or London, and seek your fortune as a screenwriter or novelist. If you're a poet, I'm sorry to say, you'd better not seek your fortune with poetry, but if you can live on fine words alone, you can move to the mountains and subsist on air. I'm joking, of course, since very few people can make it as a writer without some serious training or at least many years of apprenticeship.

The point is, you've signed up for a class in creative writing that may require you to write several different pieces in different forms. If you sit around waiting for inspiration to strike, it will get very stressful when it doesn't strike soon enough or often enough. The more stressed you are about what you haven't already written, the harder it is to write. This is often called *writer's block*, and I encounter it with students every semester. If it happens to you, talk to your instructor about it. Together, you can work through it, and it's nothing to be ashamed of.

But I am convinced that a lot of writer's block happens because of our romantic ideas of how writing ought to work, which don't match the practical realities of how most writers do work. We get these romantic notions from movies, TV, and even writers themselves, who often would rather not talk about everything that they had to go through to get that novel written and published. We get it from literature classes, where we concentrate on the final, finished product (with good reason). We analyze it for meaning and structure. We interpret. We prod and poke and try to tease out what we think the author intended (even though literary theory has argued for a century that authorial intent is elusive, unknowable, and largely irrelevant to interpretation).

We think of literature as the final product, and we imagine the author sitting down to write that final product in one fell swoop, since we often don't know the stages that went before it, and so when we sit down to write, we are impatient to get to that final product, and we want what flows from our pens or keystrokes to be that product, so we are disappointed, possibly even depressed, when it is not. But you shouldn't feel alone. This is a lesson that every writer learns and has to learn over and over again. Many novelists speak of a kind of writer's block after they finish a novel, and poets may go through the same stage after compiling a book of poems. The question of what to write is not so difficult when you have a project in mind, but when you face a new starting point, you can feel right back where you were as a young writer, staring at that blank page. Fortunately, many writers have developed strategies for overcoming this obstacle.

Process and Practice

Rather than thinking in terms of inspiration and a finished product, most successful writers think in terms of a writing process that can lead to inspiration. The fact of the matter is, the more you write, the more likely it is that you will get inspired, and if you learn where to go to find inspiration, you are more likely to encounter it on a regular basis. But if you wait for inspiration to strike you, then you are more likely to be frustrated, especially when one part of your grade depends on coming up with some good ideas. And though many people, including a few students I have known, claim to work better under pressure, I've found that nothing keeps the muse at bay better than the stress of having to come up with a good idea. Successful writers discover the process or processes that will keep them writing, even through the dry periods, when every idea feels like it's leading nowhere.

The most basic advice that most writers try to follow is to write every day. Believe me, it's not always easy or even possible to keep this resolution, especially when you're not in school and you face the demands of work and family (and occasionally having fun). It's easy to let it slide for a day or two, and it may well be unrealistic to plan to write every day. But successful writers do set aside regular times in which to write. Some write best in the morning, often getting up before dawn to write when the rest of the world isn't going to bother them; others stay up late at night or carve out some time during their lunch hour or after work in which to write.

The poet and doctor William Carlos Williams describes in his autobiography how he would write between patients. He kept a typewriter in a fold-out desk. When one patient would leave, he would flip up the typewriter and add a word or a line to the poem that was still in the roller, then flip the desk back down to hide the typewriter and call for the next patient. This system worked for him, though most of us would probably find it maddening. The point is, there is no one right routine for writing, but having a routine makes the process much easier.

If you know when you will write, it is more likely you will be mentally prepared when you sit down to do it. If you write at the same time every day or several days a week, your mind will get into the habit and the writing will flow much more easily than if there is no pattern to your writing. And yet, if your life is such that you can't establish a regular pattern and you have to write whenever you can grab a spare moment, then you have to be prepared for that as well.

Carry a notebook with you, so you can write down your thoughts when you have them. Or use your phone or tablet—writers these days have many more tools at their disposal, and those tools are a lot more portable than William Carlos Williams' typewriter desk. Make the commitment to write and write often, and the writing will come more easily.

One reason for this is that writing, like any activity, takes practice. No one would expect you to go out and run a marathon without some serious training, yet how many people think they can write a novel in a month when they haven't written anything much before that? Kudos to those who attempt it, and really high praise to anyone who finishes with even a rough draft! But the best thing about it is that it gives people an incentive to write every day for a month, and those who keep at it may get somewhere. And I suspect those who do finish a novel in a month have tried it before and have been writing already—they have been in training, in other words.

As a young writer (whatever your chronological age, if you are in an introductory creative writing class, you qualify as a young writer), your goal should be to discover the process that works for you. To do this takes practice and experimentation. You should try writing at different times of the day and in different places. You should explore many different subjects and sources of inspiration. You should challenge yourself to try new things and not rely solely on the fonts of inspiration that have worked for you in the past.

The exercises in this book are designed to do just that, and some of them will be uncomfortable and even unproductive for you (maybe they will be productive for someone else). Do them anyway! But don't worry if they don't lead to a great finished product: most won't. Give them serious effort for the duration of the exercise and any group work you do with them. Follow up with another draft to see what you might learn from the group's feedback, and then abandon the exercises that don't speak to you or work with an image or a character that does seem interesting. Once you are done with an exercise, you can do whatever you like with that writing, in other words. You can develop it further, you can change it, you can take one word from it and combine it with something else, or you can simply ignore it.

Many writers agree that in the first stages of writing you need to have absolute and total freedom. Your early writing should not be judged as good or bad: it just is. Later you will go back and see what you think is worth salvaging. Bestselling author Anne Lamott, in her seminal book on the writing process, *Bird by Bird*, spoke of writing a first "shitty draft." The point was that she wanted it to be bad in order to relieve the pressure of writing something good. If you are free to write something lousy and if you know that whatever you produce will be far from perfect, then you can write and not face writer's block.

Many young writers who face writer's block tell me that they feel whatever they write is no good. I tell them to write it anyway. If nothing else, get it out of your system, though you may find there is something of value in it once it's on paper, even if 90% of it is dross. Without the 90%, you may not ever get to the 10% that has potential, though that percent may be buried in the rest and only discovered later: it may not be the last 10%, but 1% or 2% here and there.

Your writing journal is one place for this stage of writing. If your instructor assigns a journal, as I do, then he or she may assign a grade based on whether you did enough writing, not on whether those exercises led to something good. When I grade journals, I do look at whether you gave the exercises serious effort, but not whether they are a finished product or ever could be finished.

Most of us are perfectionists, so this is a hard lesson to learn. We don't want to write something we can't use later. It seems like wasted effort. And yet it is absolutely vital to give yourself this freedom to fail and to recognize that not every word that flows from your pen will be gold. And perhaps the even harder lesson is that nearly everything you write initially will be far from its final form. These early exercises (I hesitate to even call them drafts) will take much rewriting before they become recognizable, let alone successful, as poems, stories, scripts, or essays. And that is okay. It is even normal.

In fact, it is normal for published writers, not just for neophytes. However, it does get easier the more you write: not because your early drafts are so much better, but because you train your eye to spot the good in them, and you develop a surer sense of form, so you can recognize patterns and see how to develop them more quickly. At least sometimes it feels that way! Other times, it may feel like you're starting over from square one, but at least you've been there before and you know that the final product is achievable.

Finding Form

If the first stages of writing are absolutely free and potentially even lousy, there comes a stage where you want to make something of what you've written. After all, our goal is not to write junk, but to produce something we can be proud of and that someone else might actually want to read. To take the roughest of exercises and turn it into a draft of something means finding a shape to put it in. Will it be a poem or will it be part of a story or play, for instance? Will it be long or short? Where does it begin, and what path will it take to its conclusion? Answering some of these questions, at least provisionally, will limit or expand the idea that has been started in important ways. A character sketch that I decide to develop as a poem may go on for 20 or 30 lines (or more), and may involve much more cutting than adding, though I may do some of both. A character sketch that I decide to incorporate in a story will need plot, other characters, setting, description, etc., and yet much of the sketch itself will probably go unused in the final product.

As you sculpt the form of a piece, you both add to it and cut out. You cut, not only based on what is good or bad, but also based on what fits the form you are working with. Good advice is to save the good stuff that you have to cut, but have the courage to cut it if necessary. Maybe the grandmother that didn't fit in the first story will get a story of her own, where she is part of a completely different family. The description of a sunrise that didn't fit the poem that needed to end with the eclipse of the moon might make it into another poem or might become the genesis of a story. Keep a scrapbook of these bits of writing that have been cut. Copy them into a notebook or into a file on your computer. There are even computer programs that allow you to collect clippings, sort them, categorize them, and organize them in different ways that help you manage seemingly random information.

Many of our exercises will focus on the early stage. They may ask you to write a paragraph or make a list. They may not ask you to make it a poem or a story. Later, when you decide to work on a piece, you will be able to make your own decisions about the shape you want it to take. This is done to model the process of writing described in this chapter. But as the book progresses, there will be some exercises that start with a form. These are to get you to try different forms, though again they don't have to lead to finished work. They may ask you to write a scene or to write a poem or a poem in a specific form. They might ask you to write dialogue for a play.

Because those are still early-stage exercises, you might very well re-evaluate the form and turn it into something else. Dialogue for a play might lead to a dramatic monologue poem. A scene for a story might be the genesis of a poem or play. A narrative poem might be reworked into a story, and a story might be turned into a novel or film script, though you may not be ready to tackle those big projects yet.

In other words, decisions about form don't have to be final, but choosing to try a form helps the writer to develop an idea that in its initial stages may be fairly amorphous. If one form leads to a dead end, you try another until you discover an ending you can be satisfied with. Sometimes you have to tear it all up and start over from scratch, though in this day and age, you can at least save a good copy of the last half-decent draft before you start over with a blank file or start rearranging so drastically that you might not find your way back to the draft you had.

Revision

This is what we usually think of as revision. Once an early draft has reached its endpoint or at least gotten close, so the end is nearly in sight, there comes a time to re-evaluate what has been produced. Revision is the time when you look at the form you have chosen with a fresh eye.

You look for the weak spots, and you look for the excess. You refine the form by adding and cutting as needed, and it usually takes plenty of both. You rearrange the form to find a better, more satisfying pattern. You might change from telling the story chronologically, to telling it backwards because the beginning, not the end, is where the surprise lies. You might change the line or stanza lengths in a poem or decide that what you initially wrote as one poem needs to be developed as two or three.

Revision takes a radical re-envisioning of what has been written, and too often we are satisfied with simply editing or "fixing" what we already have. This can lead to a more polished draft, but it doesn't always lead to a more successful product. If you have the courage to completely rethink what has been written, to start over and write it differently, to envision a different beginning or end, to add or remove a character or central image, to throw off the balance of what you've written until it nearly topples and then shore it up just enough that it balances on the edge, I cannot guarantee that you will come up with a better final product, but you will have two options to compare. Don't delete that half-baked file until you are sure you haven't burned it in the revision. It may take more struggle and more revision before you are satisfied, or you may go back to the original half-baked draft with new insight on how to finish it.

I suppose you could spin your wheels and never finish anything if you take revision to the extreme, but it is much more common to encounter the opposite problem. Young writers, and also many more experienced writers, are content with a draft that is polished and *written*, even if it isn't all that great. They aren't willing to take the risk of real revision, and therefore their work never reaches its full potential. Look at the difference between first novels, that often take years to write and get published, and second novels that sometimes get dashed off because the publisher wants a sequel. That first novel can be finely crafted because the author labored over it and revised it multiple times after every rejection from a publisher or agent. The second novel may be sloppier and less developed simply because there wasn't the time and the incentive to revise as extensively. Of course, this doesn't happen to every novelist, but you see it often enough to witness the value of revision and to sympathize with those novelists working under tight deadlines.

In other words, revision is not just editing or proofreading. Editing involves making relatively minor changes to paragraphs or maybe sentence structure. It might involve some cutting and pasting or rearranging, but it doesn't drastically alter the form or shape of the piece. Proofreading means correcting for grammar and spelling. Both are important parts of the final polishing, and you need to do them. But revision involves a global assessment of a piece of writing. It involves major change, and often involves coming up with new characters or new ideas, generating significant new writing and cutting out significant passages that aren't necessary to the final piece.

A Recursive Process

It would be nice if the process of writing went just the way I have described it above: if you started with rough and raw material, found something of value in it, gave it a shape, and refined it into a finished product. That sounds like a process with a guaranteed output. All you have to do is follow the steps. And sometimes it happens like that. But often the process is not so straightforward; instead it is recursive. This means that it is a cycle. The early stages of pure invention may lead to a form, but in exploring that form, you will need to come up with new material to fill it, thus going back to the invention or even inspiration stage. In the process of revision, you will likely reassess the form you chose initially. You completely reshape it, rather than simply refine it, and this involves more invention. They are not separate steps of a straightforward process, in other words; they are interwoven aspects of a process that is often messy and even frustrating, but in the end it can be very rewarding.

The main thing to know now is that the process is almost guaranteed to be messy. That way, when you are stuck in the middle of it, and you can't find your way out, you will know that this is what you should expect. It isn't because you are a lousy writer and should never have tried to write the piece you're stuck on (though it's easy to convince yourself of that), but it is part of the process that every writer must go through at least some if not most of the time, and there is light at the end of the tunnel. Even if you feel you need to scrap everything and start over.

It is a little like the potter whose vase crumples as he or she was just reaching the rim. Maybe there was a bubble in the clay or the potter's hand moved imperceptibly in the wrong direction at the wrong time. He or she discards that mass of clay or recycles it and begins again, but this time with the sense memory of two vases in his or her hands: one is the vase that crumpled and the other is of the vase that will stand. This second vase will probably be thrown more easily and it has a better chance of coming out as intended because the potter has learned from the previous flawed attempt.

In the same way, I firmly believe that every draft has value, even those that never reach a finished state. As long as we as writers take them seriously and revise until we are sure they can't be salvaged or put them away until we see the way to reach a successful revision, even our failed attempts or the roughest drafts can lead us on to the next idea (or the next) that will be successful.

A large part of what you are doing is gaining practice in creative writing. I doubt you will earn a Nobel Prize for anything you write at this point, but you will gain experience with the process of writing, you will learn more about its forms, and you will discover new options to explore. And in the end, you should produce a portfolio of which you can be proud and some of which you might try to publish in your university literary magazine or other local or regional magazines.

You will have learned a lot about how literature gets written, and you will have taken another step on your path toward becoming a serious writer, if that is one of your goals.

✒ Writing Journal Exercises

1. Free write for at least 10 minutes. Try not to think too much about what you are writing, just write whatever comes to mind. Don't worry about form. What you write does not have to be a story or poem, though it can be the beginnings of something. It does not have to be

about any one thing. Try to fill the first page with whatever you have to write about, even if that is that you aren't sure what to write. You will have filled a page and your journal won't be completely blank. That is your only goal. If something interesting happens while you're writing, great, but if not, that's all right.

2. Make a list of subjects you might like to write about. Try to be as specific as possible—rather than writing "family," list some family members or aspects of family life that you could write about. Next make a list of subjects you are unlikely to write about. Again, try to be specific. Don't just write "war" or "politics."

3. Choose a subject that you think you are unlikely to write about. Write for five minutes on that subject. It doesn't have to be great writing. You can list things about it that you don't like or describe the worst aspects of it. Try to keep writing until you find something you might like to write about, despite yourself.

4. Choose a subject that you think you would like to write about. Find some objects, pictures, music, etc. that remind you of that subject. Set these around your writing area (or turn on the music) and write for 5 or 10 minutes. Don't worry about what you're writing, just free write any ideas that come to mind.

5. Take your journal to a place where you have never written before. It might be a new coffee shop or student lounge. It might be outdoors or it might be at the bowling alley. If it is in a classroom, try to do your writing before or after class. Write for five minutes or more about whatever comes to mind. Try not to stop writing. Don't think about what to write, just write based on what you see around you or based on your own inner thoughts.

6. If you are having trouble starting any of these exercises with words, start drawing instead. Keep your pen or pencil on the page as much as possible. Don't worry whether your drawing is a picture or a blob, just feel the texture of the paper and the movement of your hand as you doodle. Let the pen form words. It doesn't matter what they are. Respond to the shape of your drawing or write something completely unrelated.

3

Language, Rhythm, and Sound

Language

In the next several chapters, we will begin our exploration of writing by discussing some of the basic building blocks of the writer's trade. These are the essential tools we work with, and they can be a source of inspiration. So what better place to start than with language itself?

Most writers are obsessed with language, and for good reason. Language is the essential medium in which writers work. Painters have to learn about their tools of paint, brushes, and canvas or other surfaces, sketch artists learn to work with different pencils and the textures of paper, sculptors learn the properties of clay or stone or metal, and musicians learn the qualities of sound, the sequences of scales and chords, as well as the physical properties of their chosen instrument. Writers work with words and sentences, so it is no wonder that we pay close attention to their meaning and to their more physical properties of tone and rhythm.

It may seem odd to focus on language, though. After all, we are all adults and have been speaking one language or another for nearly two decades, possibly longer. We have heard language since the moment we were born, and we can use it without consciously thinking. And yet, precisely because language is so familiar, we as writers need to take time to consider how we use it, even if sometimes we rely on instinct and just let it rip. This is much like the painter who has seen colors all of her life: when she first begins to paint, she must relearn what happens when colors combine or are put next to each other. But it seems more obvious that you would have to learn the properties of pigments and paints than that you might need to stop and think about the way language sounds or even creates meaning.

Think of it this way: every one of you probably has a vocabulary of several thousand words—estimates range from 5,000 to 50,000 or more. The Oxford English Dictionary lists around 600,000 words, so it is extremely unlikely that any one person knows them all, especially since some are archaic forms that are no longer actively in use. The total number of words that you can recognize is considered your *passive vocabulary*. But the total number of words that you actually use on a regular basis is considered your *active vocabulary*. If you think about it, that number will likely be much smaller than your passive vocabulary.

So there are different ways to improve your vocabulary. The first is what we usually think of and what is marketed on word-a-day calendars or websites: learning the meanings of new, often obscure words. There's nothing wrong with this strategy, and it can be a fun activity, though if that's not your cup of tea, then you may be glad that there are alternatives. One of the best ways to improve your vocabulary is by using the dictionary while you read whenever you encounter a word you don't know, especially if the meaning isn't clear from the context. You can also increase your active vocabulary by using more words that you already know every day.

Playing word games like Scrabble and Boggle or doing crossword puzzles might help. That's also one of the benefits of frequent writing: you jog your memory and practice using words in new combinations. Whether you are writing something that you know you will continue to work on, or whether you are practicing free writing or simply writing down lists of words associated with a certain topic, you are actively engaging in language, which will help you expand your active vocabulary and allow those words to come to mind when you need them.

How many times have you struggled to find the right word or felt it was on the tip of your tongue? I can't guarantee that this will never happen if you write actively every day, but it stands to reason that it will happen less as your active vocabulary increases. Often when we can't find the right word, there is another, more familiar word that seems to stand in its way. This word may not have the exact shade of meaning or the sound that you want. It may just not "feel" right or we have the sneaking suspicion that there is a better word just around the corner.

This is a situation when a *thesaurus* can come in handy, though I always raise this option with a fair amount of trepidation. We all know the kind of writer who sounds like he or she overuses the thesaurus. Every word has multiple syllables and many seem to be used in the wrong context, as if the writer wasn't really familiar with the word. The language sounds ponderous and dead, rather than fresh and alive. Be careful when you use a word from a thesaurus and make sure that you understand its meaning thoroughly. Don't just look up the definition: live with it for a while, see it used in context, become utterly familiar with it before you appropriate it for your own use. And beware of the dictionary style thesaurus that only lists a few synonyms for each word.

A much better choice is a conceptual thesaurus like the old-fashioned *Roget's*, which is organized by concept, rather than by word. You look up the word you know in the index, then go to the concepts it is listed in. There you will find many more options than in a dictionary thesaurus, and none of them will be exact synonyms. No word is the exact equivalent of another word, anyway, so it helps if the range is wider. Often the word you can think of is a few steps away from the one you want, and the thesaurus can remind you of a word whose meaning is close, but not exactly the same. Every writer should own or have access to a good thesaurus and a good dictionary that are easy and comfortable to use. As with anything, personal preference can be important, so use the tools that work best for you.

As you choose the right word, you of course want to choose a word with the right *denotation*, or a definition that fits the concept you are thinking of. However, for many concepts there are multiple words that mean nearly the same thing with only slight shades of difference. Often when picking the right word, we are also looking for a word with the right *connotations*. Maybe a word has multiple meanings, and though the primary meaning we understand from the context is accurate, its connotations may be fortunate or unfortunate. Sometimes a word suggests a particular context or is used by a certain class or in specific situations. The word "lasso," for instance, calls up images of cowboys or rodeos, even if it is used in a more modern setting for throwing a rope around any object that isn't a steer, and photo editors use a lasso tool. Writers play with the meaning of words, and use one word to suggest another. The most blatant form of this kind of word play is called a *pun*. You may not want to write puns that will make your reader groan, but that kind of playfulness with language often is rewarding.

Rhythm

We have been talking about individual words, yet language is made up of words in a sequence. Individually, words don't always carry much meaning, and even when they do, the lack of surrounding words gives them emphasis. Typically, we write in sentences, though there are creative uses of fragments, lists, or other structures. *Syntax*, the order of words in a sequence, has an effect on the feeling, even the meaning of language. The length of a sentence even makes a difference.

Some writers use simple, declarative sentences. Others write in long flowing sentences that string together multiple clauses stretching out the meaning and looking at their subjects from many different angles before they finally reach their conclusions. There is no one right way to write a good sentence, and most writers strive for some level of variety in their syntax. Many writers edit their sentences extensively until they have not only the right words, but also the right length and the right order to communicate the literal meaning as well as the right connotation and feeling to the reader.

Sentence pattern is one way to think about rhythm in language. Syntax makes a big difference. If you write in long, complicated sentences that ebb and flow, then your sentences will have one kind of rhythm. Short, declarative sentences give a different feeling. This can be emphasized by repeating certain phrases or grammatical structures. A common form is called *anaphora*, which is the term for a repeated initial word or phrase. If each sentence in a list repeats all or part of the opening phrase, it creates a chant-like feeling. Psalms and hymns often make use of this technique.

The opposite, repetition of a word or phrase at the end of a sentence or line, is called *epistrophe*. Like anaphora, epistrophe adds emphasis to the repeated elements. There are other rhetorical terms for types of repetition you might explore on your own, but these two are a good place to start. Though they can be (and often are) used in prose, they are often associated with poetry.

Everyone knows that a comma indicates a slight pause, and a period indicates a bigger pause, as does a colon and a semicolon or dash. Even without a comma, we may pause slightly before some phrases. There may be more of a pause between a noun and the prepositional phrase that follows it than there is between a noun and a verb or between a preposition and its object. Every time we speak, there is a natural ebb and flow to our language. Syntax, aided by punctuation, is one way any writer can make note of and attempt to control it. Of course, no two readers will read the same passage in exactly the same way, so total control is elusive.

Another way to think about rhythm in language is to think in terms of accent or stress. English is classified as an *accentual language* as opposed to classical Greek, which is a *quantitative language*. In a quantitative language, rhythm is determined by the length of the syllables, since a long vowel actually takes more time to pronounce than a short one. In English, long and short vowels have approximately the same length but the sound varies. So instead of organizing rhythm by long and short syllables, in English and other accentual languages, we consider whether a syllable is stressed or unstressed. A stressed syllable will be slightly louder than an unstressed syllable.

Most dictionaries mark the stressed syllables in the pronunciation guide for a word with an accent mark. If you listen to a word or series of words, you can hear where the accents fall, though I will admit that this can be a little difficult, especially for students whose education hasn't emphasized meter. One reason it can be hard to hear is that there are more than two levels of accent in English. Some linguists have identified three or more levels of stress, and of course the term "unstressed" could be seen as a misnomer. If a syllable had absolutely no stress, it would be silent. What we call an unstressed syllable has less stress than the surrounding syllables, and sometimes it may depend on the context—what level of stress the surrounding syllables have—and the performance, whether someone places extra emphasis on a word or part of a word. For example: the articles "a" and "the" may be stressed or even pronounced differently, depending on the context or performance. Still, in general people tend to pronounce words with the correct stress and recognize when words are pronounced incorrectly. If I said it like this—INcorrectLY—you would recognize that it should be pronounced—incorrECTly.

But I have noticed that students have a hard time hearing stress, which is why I want to introduce the concept now and save a discussion of meter (which uses stress to organize a line) for the chapter on poetry. Rather than worrying right now about the technical terms for rhythms in formal verse, pay attention to the rhythms in your writing, whether you are writing in poetry or prose. Listen to the rise and fall of accents across a sentence and the pattern of sentences in a paragraph in prose. Try to find an interesting rhythm for the lines of your poem. Find patterns and look for ways to repeat those patterns. If you begin that now, then when we get to meter, the technical terms may begin to make more sense.

Sound

Another aspect of language that is often equated with poetry is *rhyme*. In fact, when we get to poetry, I want to look at rhyme and other ways to structure the sound of a poem, so here I want to introduce some ideas about sound that can be applied to any kind of writing. Though poets may pay closer attention to the sound of their words, fiction writers, essayists, and playwrights consider sound when choosing the right word for a given context.

A basic definition of rhyme might be "pairs of words that sound alike." But of course, rhyme words usually don't have identical sounds. In fact, some systems of rhyme would disallow identical-sounding words (like "I" and "eye") as being too close to constitute rhyme. Other systems would allow it. This varies from language to language and from time to time: the conventions of rhyme evolve and change just like any other convention, and arguably in the twenty-first century those conventions are fairly loose, depending on who your audience is and what they will accept, of course.

Typically, rhyme words have the same ending sounds. The first part of the final syllable is different, but the final sounds are the same—"cat" and "hat," for instance. This is often called *true rhyme* or *perfect rhyme*. Variations on true rhyme are called *off rhyme* or *slant rhyme*. In these cases the vowel might be slightly different, yet still similar enough to be recognized ("hot" and "nut," for instance). Like beauty, off rhyme or slant rhyme can be in the eye or ear of the beholder, and some people distinguish between off and slant rhyme by degree, though there isn't universal agreement about which is further from true rhyme: off rhyme or slant rhyme. There are a few other terms that amount to about the same thing, but these are the two most common.

Rhyme does not have to be only one syllable. Usually in English, true rhyme includes the last stressed syllable and any unstressed syllables that follow it, so SYLLable would rhyme with BILLable, but not necessarily with ABle, since the vowel sound and the stress is off. Some might allow it as a slant rhyme or off rhyme variant, though. Some writers revel in multisyllabic rhyme, even rhyming several words with one polysyllabic word. For examples, pick up just about any poem by Lord Byron, especially "Don Juan," where he uses multisyllabic rhyme for ironic and quite humorous effect.

Besides rhyme, there are other ways to structure the sound of your language. Repetition of any sounds heightens the interest or, if overdone, adds to the humor, potentially. If really overdone, it can even become annoying. *Alliteration* is one familiar technique that involves repeating the initial sounds of words. Some people only consider the repetition of initial consonants as alliteration (e.g. two ticklish turtles trying to tango), but others, myself among them, consider initial vowels alliterative as well (e.g. any actors adding apples and artichokes). Probably two or three words that alliterate at a time are plenty unless you're writing a book for early readers or you are trying for humorous or annoying effect!

Similarly, the repetition of any consonant sound across a string of words can pattern it. This is called *consonance*, and the consonant sounds do not have to come at the beginning of the word, they can come in the middle or at the end. Some definitions of consonance disallow the use of initial consonants, though that seems somewhat arbitrary. As long as most of the repeated sounds are in the middle or at the end, then it won't sound like alliteration. Similarly, *assonance* is the repetition of vowel sounds in a passage.

Some linguists have argued that the repetition of certain sounds has an effect on the meaning of a passage, so that the use of dark "o" or "u" sounds may make a passage sound more mysterious or sad, whereas the use of brighter "i" or "ee" sounds may make a passage happier. The problem is that this isn't invariably the case. Some sad words have bright vowels, for instance. Meaning and sound interact across a sentence or a line, and neither one fully counteracts the effect of the other. But there is no denying that sound makes a difference in our response to a passage, even if we can't precisely quantify its effect. Similarly, most people will experience some consonants as percussive and others as more liquid or smooth. Though it's hard to predict exactly what the effect of certain consonants might be on a passage, it's equally hard to prove that they don't have an effect.

So writers tend not to listen to linguists when it comes to sound and language (though it can be fun to read linguists and to theorize), but instead they write by ear. Choosing the word combinations that sound good to your own ear is likely the best way to go. Reading other writers with an ear to how their prose or poetry sounds can help you learn to pay attention to sound in your writing. Reading your own work aloud can also help you hear the sound of it.

When we write an essay for a class, we typically pay much more attention to the meaning of the words. After all, our primary goal is to convey information. This is also true of most everyday speech. However, a professional speech writer often pays close attention to rhythm and sound, since they are important ways to emphasize meaning and to get the emotional appeal across to the crowd. Creative writers aren't alone in these concerns, in other words, but we do pay more attention to them in our creative writing than we do in other contexts. I will venture to say, though, that once you start paying attention to rhythm and sound, it may begin to affect even the way you draft a quick email.

The best way to begin working with language, rhythm, and sound is the same as with any early-stage writing. The best advice, once you have identified some strategies you would like to use, is to play. Try writing in a rhythm or try overdoing it with alliteration, assonance, consonance, or rhyme. You aren't trying to create a finished product; you are learning to pay attention to the richness of language and develop an ear for sound and rhythm that you can use later when you are polishing a final draft.

Some writers start with something to say, an idea to convey or a topic they want to explore. Many creative writers begin with language, with a phrase that gets stuck in their head or with a conversation they have overheard. They don't have a meaning in mind when they set out, but they let language unfold as they go. They explore different patterns and sounds. They follow connections between words. They discover meaning through language as they work on a draft, and in doing so, they are able to say more than they thought they even knew. Sometimes writers scare themselves with what they are able to say. Sometimes they impress themselves at the insights they uncover. Often they get pleasure from language in the writing, long before they reach a final draft, and the pleasure of bringing it all together in a satisfying form may be the one goal all artists share. As writers, language is our medium, and our joy. Our task is to explore it through all its levels of meaning, rhythm, and sound.

✒ Writing Journal Exercises

1. Try writing a paragraph that sounds like the rhythm an animal makes when it moves. Consider the rhythms of the sentences and the sounds of the consonants. Should the sounds of the words be sharp and percussive or smooth and slippery? Should the sentences be long and convoluted or short and choppy? Don't worry what the sentences mean—they don't have to describe the animal's movements (though they can). Instead, try to get at the rhythms and sounds of the animal even if you're writing about something else.

2. Start with a phrase like "I traded this for that" or "If this, then that" or "Because this, there was that," "Whenever this happens, then that happens," etc. Repeat the phrase with variations, changing the this and the that each time, explaining why the action occurs some of the time or finding other ways to change the pattern somewhat before coming back to it again.

3. Write your own thesaurus entry for a concept. Start with a general concept like "sky" or "city," and list as many words as you can for that concept. You may use brief phrases, like "blue sky" or "mean streets." List verbs associated with the concept and adjectives or adverbs. Then get more specific. List words for parts of the general concept: names of clouds or names of streets or buildings. Try to find surprising words and common expressions or regionalisms.

4. Write lists of rhyme words. Try writing two- or three-syllable rhymes. Look for surprising combinations, and move beyond true rhyme to include slant rhyme or off rhyme. Consider syllables within a word that rhyme with another word (such as "intend" that rhymes with "commend-able"). Try to include at least 10 words in each list, but don't worry about whether individual words make sense together.

5. Write a list of as many colloquial expressions as you can think of. Either write a list of the phrases you grew up hearing or write a list of phrases that you have heard in new settings, which struck you as interesting or odd because they were unfamiliar.

6. Write a sound poem. You may write it in lines or write it as a prose paragraph. Write out words that sound interesting when put next to one another, but which don't make any logical sense. Don't worry about grammar or syntax, though if your sentences do follow normal grammar, make sure the word combinations don't make sense for very long. Feel free to invent words simply for their sounds or their rhythms. Think of "The Jabberwocky" as one model.

7. Make lists of words associated with a subject. This could be lists of words associated with a setting or a profession, or it could be lists of colors, sounds, types of animals or plants, etc. If you want to write about a subject, it can be useful to write lists of words associated with the subject, since this could jog your memory or spark your imagination. Don't just list nouns, by the way.

8. Try writing a list of verbs for a particular activity. And don't be satisfied with a list of three or four words. Keep writing until you've exhausted the subject, then consider doing some research to add to your list.

4

The Writer in the World

Raw Materials and Rules

We have discussed the writing process and we've begun to look at the most fundamental aspect of writing: language. Over the next few chapters, we'll be looking at more of the raw materials writers draw on for inspiration, as we continue to look at the fundamentals that go into all good writing. This may be a good time to take a moment to think about the "rules" of creative writing. Some textbooks are organized around rules for good writing, though in general I try to avoid talking in terms of rules or in terms of what's right and what's wrong. When discussing rules, I prefer to think of them in terms of conventions—the expectations a reader is likely to have when reading in a literary genre. Some are genre specific and others hold true for any creative writing, regardless of form. As with any expectation, it is always possible to defy literary conventions, but it is helpful to know what they are so you know when you are bucking a trend and when you are following it. In the pages to come, when we discuss "what good writers do" or "what the conventions are," you should realize that "good writers" sometimes break all the "rules," but they typically know what they are doing and why. Taken in this spirit, the rules of good writing are more like ground rules or, as I like to think of them, fundamentals. Sure you can do something different, as long as you have good reason to. And if that catches on, then it may become the new rule or convention.

So far we have looked at the writing process, and I have described the way many writers say they write. We also noted that every writer is individual, and you have to find the process that works well for you. This takes plenty of experimentation, especially in the early stages. We have also talked about language, one of the raw materials of writing that is impossible to avoid. In the coming chapters, we will examine more fundamentals and raw materials that most writers rely on: some more than others. These are places you might go for inspiration, as well as the basics that any writer is likely to deal with on a day-to-day basis. And these are aspects of writing that are common to all genres: fiction, poetry, nonfiction, or drama.

Observation

Aside from language itself, one of the first places many writers look for inspiration or the stuff of their writing is the world around them. I know that for the university student this may seem uninspiring. After all, who wants to read yet another story about campus life—plenty of people, so don't let me dissuade you if that's what you had in mind! But when I say you can write about the world around you, I don't necessarily mean your immediate surroundings. Anywhere you can get to is still your world. Many writers go exploring for inspiration, whether that means taking a trip or searching out new locales in their immediate area. Most students are somewhat limited in how far they can travel, but you can get off campus to look for other settings, and even on campus there is plenty of material to work with. So for this chapter, let's limit ourselves to observing the world around us, though in the coming chapters we'll expand on that strategy.

How much goes unnoticed in your world every day? Even if you don't take a trip or go to a place you usually don't frequent, even if you are in your room or on your way to class, there are a million things you probably don't look at or think about. Consider the smallest things you can see in your world. Look at a blade of grass up close or examine the bark of a tree. If you're not a naturalist, you might pay just as close attention to the details of a car or the cracks in the sidewalk or ceiling. What patterns do the shadows of the leaves make? How does the light appear in a quiet room lit only by a naked bulb in the ceiling when the night outside is completely silent and the solitary person in the room is certain he has heard an intruder at the door? What sounds can you hear as you walk to class? What kinds of trees are there on campus and what are the differences between them? Is the shade of a gingko tree the same as that of a cypress? In which seasons? What scents or textures, even tastes, are there in your surroundings? There's no need to limit yourself to the pleasant experiences—writers need to describe the dark and unpleasant things in life as well.

Become a keen observer of the physical world you inhabit and learn how to talk and write about it. Learn the names of plants and animals around you. Learn the terminology for describing their structures: what is the difference between a pistil and a stamen? Which animals have a snout and which have a muzzle? What kinds of bark are found on trees? A field guide can be an invaluable source of names and information. But it is not just the natural world that needs description.

Consider a mechanic's garage. What are the names of all the tools and all of their parts? What types of grease or soap get used? How does it feel or smell? What do you call the many parts of a lamp or table in an antique store? What are the proper names for the decorative ornaments on a staircase or on the walls of a building? How do you name its columns or the types of windows or gables? What are the proper or common names of kitchen utensils, pots, and pans? How do cooks describe temperature?

A good writer pays close attention to the world and mines it for details that might be used in a story or poem. Yet language is still part of that mix. How do you describe the color of a cardinal (or should you call it a red bird, especially if you live in the American South)? How do you describe the sound it makes? Don't limit yourself only to the physical world around you. Pay attention to the people you see as well. What do they look like, what do they wear, and how do they move? Listen to the way people talk. There is so much material all around you that you hardly need to go a mile from your home to have something to write about.

Language is the great mediator between humans and their world. Some linguists theorize that without language humans wouldn't be able to think (though some people believe that animals think without language or with their own languages, such as bird calls). Whether or not thought is possible without language, it's clear that, for humans, we primarily think in language. Perhaps the first words were used for naming things: nouns. These were probably followed quickly by verbs to name what things do and qualifiers, adjectives and adverbs, to help describe how. From there, you get simple sentences, and even though human language has evolved to the point that we can discuss very abstract concepts (like how to write), that basis in naming still seems to be the core of our experience of language.

Image

This basis of language in experience may be one reason the *image* remains one of the most basic elements of clear writing. The use of concrete, visual terms to portray a subject is so ingrained in our ideas about good writing that it has led to the common dictum: "Show, don't tell." Of course, this may be a little extreme. Some telling can be a more efficient strategy: why not just come out and say what you mean, after all? Many writers have altered this advice to something along the lines of: "Tell by showing." William Carlos Williams put it famously: "No ideas but in things." Typically, in creative writing, telling by itself is not enough.

Readers want to experience the world that a writer imagines, not just hear about it secondhand. Think about any good story or poem you have read recently. What are the most memorable parts? Probably you are thinking about a strong image, the characters, or a setting. You may feel that you can see the action unfolding right before your eyes, though of course you may not "see" the exact images that the author had in mind. How often were you disappointed when reading children's literature to form an idea about a character and then find an illustration halfway through the book that did not match the way you had imagined her?

Yet writers have also struggled with the idea of the image. Even Ezra Pound, one of the founders and early promoters of the Modernist school of poetry called Imagism, qualified the idea of the image after a while, calling it "an emotional construct." Later he would go on to form the competing movement of Vorticism, both due to poetic rivalries and out of a sense that pure Imagism lacked energy and dynamism. Rather than a static description, writers recognize a need for the image to include motion. Rather than limiting the image to the sense of sight, most writers have included all the senses in their concept of an image; some call it a sense image to make this clear. Writers recognize that, to be most effective, an image must be moving, in terms of both moving through space and being emotionally moving.

Writers make use of language, a very abstract system of marks on a surface that represent the sound of words, to call up a mental image in the reader. In many ways, this is a magical experience. Most other artists use a concrete medium (paints, clay, ink, or the human body for dance) to portray an image. Music uses sound, and may be even more abstract than writing, since its sounds evoke emotion, but it does not use language to convey meaning (unless there are lyrics, which arguably are a form of poetry). The world that a writer creates can move in time and space; it can present smells and sounds and even touch or taste. It can seem more real even than a movie to the reader who is transported to the world of the story or poem and feels like he or she is experiencing it. All thanks to our ability to imagine the vivid sensory images we encounter in the written text.

Metaphor

Striking sensory images may be the basis of most good writing, yet writers do also work with meaning: we generally have something to say. How can these two strategies work together? One way is through the use of comparison. Sometimes writers rely on *juxtaposition* of images to imply a comparison. They simply place images next to one another and allow the reader to make the connections. This strategy can be useful if you don't want to determine how the reader will interpret the image. It allows for *ambiguity* and multiple interpretations.

But there are times when you want to limit the reader's interpretations, too. Then you may want a specific kind of comparison, or you may want to guide the reader by spelling out how two things compare. The general term for using images to make a comparison is metaphor, though some people divide comparison into two main types: *metaphor* (comparison of different things) and *metonymy* (equation of similar things).

Metonymy is using a related image to refer to something else: for instance, calling the police "men in blue" because of the color of their uniforms would be metonymy.

Synecdoche is a form of metonymy that uses a part to refer to the whole: for example, the term "heads of state" and the phrase "all hands on deck" use synecdoche to name leaders and sailors respectively.

Either technique can be used as a kind of shorthand, and it can be fun, adding ornament to your language. Many common idioms make use of this kind of wordplay and are part of our everyday speech. Listen carefully to the speech of the people around you, and you are likely to pick up on lively phrases, called *idioms*. Often the most fascinating use of language comes from regional expressions. You don't necessarily have to create new idioms, but knowing when and how to employ them helps give your writing life.

More common tropes in literature are types of metaphor. You have probably learned the distinction between *metaphor* and *simile*. These are both literary terms for comparisons, which are easy to distinguish because *simile* uses "like" or "as," but *metaphor* uses "is." The difference is greater than the words that get used, though. Simile identifies a similarity between two things; metaphor establishes identity. If I say that the sky is as blue as the ocean, then only the blueness is similar. If I say the sky is like the ocean, the reader discovers similarities when I go on to say how they are alike. But if I say, "The sky is an ocean; let me dive in and swim," then suddenly the whole idea of sky changes: perhaps hawks become dolphins and the clouds breakers. You could elaborate that description and create a whole poem around it.

Metaphor tends to be more direct and immediate, more intense, so the common wisdom has often been to use metaphor in preference to simile most of the time. Still, I have always questioned that advice. There's nothing wrong with a good simile, and in some poems the sky isn't the ocean, but is similar to it. Knowing the difference and deciding when you want the intensity of metaphor and when a simile is more appropriate seems to be the best course.

An *analogy* is an extended simile, where you go into detail about how two things are similar. They may also be very dissimilar in other aspects, but you point out similarities. Usually, the point of an analogy is to gain some insight into one of those things. When Shakespeare in "Sonnet 18" compares his love to a summer day, it is not just to say that she has a sunny disposition, but to remind us that her youth and beauty will not last; there will be trials and storms, and eventually summer will be replaced by winter (old age or death), yet his poem preserves her beauty and saves her from the fate of summer.

> Shall I compare thee to a summer's day?
> Thou art more lovely and more temperate.
> Rough winds do shake the darling buds of May,
> And summer's lease hath all too short a date.
> Sometime too hot the eye of heaven shines,
> And often is his gold complexion dimmed;
> And every fair from fair sometime declines,
> By chance, or nature's changing course, untrimmed;
> But thy eternal summer shall not fade,
> Nor lose possession of that fair thou ow'st,
> Nor shall death brag thou wander'st in his shade,
> When in eternal lines to time thou grow'st.
> So long as men can breathe, or eyes can see,
> So long lives this, and this gives life to thee.

When you go into great detail with metaphor, we call it an *extended metaphor*. As with the general terms, it is useful to know when to extend the metaphor or make an analogy out of a simile. It is also good to know when to stop!

In literature, we also use other terms for specific kinds of comparisons. *Symbol* can be used as the general term, like metaphor, for any kind of symbolism. Often though, it is used for a specific use of an image to represent something else, usually an idea. The term comes from a Greek word which derives from the two halves of a coin that were used to cement an agreement: each party would take one half. So a symbol is when an image in a story or poem represents a larger, more abstract concept that typically is not named in the story or poem. A rose might symbolize love (though that might be a little trite).

A similar concept is *allegory*, where an image also represents something outside the text. Generally, an allegory involves a system of images or characters that represent ideas or in the case of a political allegory that represent people or classes in real life. A political allegory might be used to criticize a government without naming names (and getting in serious trouble). A religious allegory might use characters to represent ideas on morality or faith.

Personification means giving human qualities to animals, inanimate objects, or abstractions. It is a little like analogy or allegory, though unlike allegory, it may not be quite as complex a system of comparisons. Aesop's fables use personification, since animals act like humans and are used to criticize human behaviors. A less elaborate use of personification might be seen in a description, where the writer simply says "the wind played with her hair." Of course, wind can't play, but we see it better with this description, and it gives the scene a lighter quality than "the wind blew her hair around."

We tend to think of metaphor as linking similar things, but sometimes it can be used to link opposites, resulting in a *paradox*. The English poet John Keats identified the extended use of paradox as *negative capability*, which he thought of as the ability of a poem to present opposite images or emotions without resolving their contradictions. Though the term negative capability usually is applied to poetry, the concept could be used in fiction or other forms of writing as well. The intensity of the image is increased by the contrast between the two qualities. A phrase that accomplishes this same feat is called an *oxymoron*; for example, "going at a slow speed" seems to be an oxymoron.

Another way to combine different things is to mingle the senses or to describe one sense in terms of another. This is called *synesthesia*, and is often used for the senses that are harder to describe, such as scent or taste. A food might be said to have a hot flavor or a sharp aftertaste, for instance. Writers can make creative use of synesthesia to add intensity to their images.

Any of these techniques can be used to get at the qualities in the world around us that are difficult to put into words. Often it takes a combination of images or a comparison between two things to get just the right shade of meaning across. At other times the use of these tropes has more to do with finding a new and interesting way to say it than with accurately depicting the outside world. Or the goal may be to be both accurate and interesting. Whatever they do, though, writers typically try to avoid the *cliché*: dry, overused phrases that are more catchphrases than vibrant images, or symbols that have been done to death. There are exceptions to this "rule," though. If a character speaks in clichés, it may be a character trait, or if a writer uses the cliché in a new context or takes it literally and causes the reader to see it in a new light, then it might be justified. As with any rule, if you can break it constructively, then go for it!

❧ Writing Journal Exercises

1. Go to a public place and write down everything you see, hear, smell, taste, and touch. Make a list for each of the five senses. Include as many words as you can, associated with the sensory perceptions in that place. Do not write in complete sentences; use single words or phrases. Then write a paragraph about the place, drawing on as many words from your lists as possible.
2. Pick a day and pick one of your senses other than sight: focus on that sense. Try to record as many different perceptions as possible. For each of those perceptions, note the time, place, and any memories or associations you have with it.
3. Pick an animal or plant. List three abstract qualities you associate with it (or part of it). Then list two places you expect to find it and two places you'd be surprised to find it. Then consider who witnesses it in that place and what else may be going on in the scene. Write a paragraph describing the plant or animal and try to evoke one of its qualities. You may focus on the original image of a plant or animal, or you may focus on the bigger picture of the surrounding scene.
4. Find a small object, preferably something natural like a leaf, a piece of driftwood, or a pine cone, or if it is man-made, then something

simple, non-mechanical. In about half a page, describe the object in detail, using only concrete, specific, sensory words, no abstractions.

5. Find an unfamiliar item, something you've found in a closet, garage, or an antique store or thrift store, for example. It should be something that doesn't belong to you and that you haven't used. You might not even recognize what it is. In about half a page, describe the object in detail, using only concrete, specific, sensory words, no abstractions.

6. Describe the small object you wrote about in one of the previous two assignments again, but this time use figurative language. You might treat the object itself as a symbol for an abstract idea or you might compare different aspects of it to other things (or concepts) using metaphor or simile. Or you might personify the object or use one of the other figures of speech.

7. Notice something or someone moving. It may be a large motion like a car driving by or a windmill turning, or it may be a small motion like windshield wipers or a child writing with a crayon. Describe the motion in detail. Include not only the way the motion looks, but the sounds it creates or the feeling it gives. If there is a scent or taste associated with it, include that as well. Describe it over time. How does the quality of the motion, or how do the other sensory perceptions associated with it, change.

5

Past Worlds

Memory

In the previous chapter, we have talked about writing from experience, paying attention to the world around and relying on the concrete, specific images you see, hear, feel, smell, or taste. I said at the outset that you might find this limiting if you feel you can only write about your campus, and though you can extend your world by going off campus, you may not be able to travel far enough, especially during the term. One place to go for inspiration, especially if you can't travel far, is to the past. We begin our discussion of this in the most accessible place: your own memory.

Consider for a moment your earliest childhood memories. What was your first house like? It may be the only house your family ever lived in, or you may have moved around. Still, the house as it was when you were four or five is likely very different from the house you live in today. As you think about the sofa you had in the living room (or was it a couch in a family room?) or the bedspread you lay across to read books from the library, you likely have a strong emotional response. There may be other things you remember that affect you more than these examples.

Often a scent or a flavor will transport you back to a time when you had that experience before. Or a confluence of sights can remind you of another time or place. Sometimes this feeling is so strong we call the experience *déjà vu*, as if we've been someplace before, when we know we haven't. We may not recognize exactly where we know it from, but a memory is triggered in our minds.

It is this strong connection with memory that makes the past such a fruitful place for inspiration. Some writers spend much of their careers writing about their childhoods. You may not wish to go back to your earliest memories, but it is likely that there is a time in your life that will speak to you. Think of that time. How much can you remember? The more time you spend with those memories, the more details are likely to come to mind. As with writing about the present, using concrete, specific images will bring back the intensity of the experience and carry it across to your reader. The more specific you can be, the more likely your readers are to visualize what you're writing about, and the experience of it will allow them to relate. Generalizations rarely pack the same kind of punch.

Yet memory also reminds us that no writer can possibly include every detail of a setting or character. Memory is selective. You remember the moments that have emotional impact, even if you may not always realize why they are important to you. The details about each moment that you remember are the ones that left an impression, even if at times they may feel random now. You remember the bedspread in your childhood room, but you may not remember the table lamp beside the bed as clearly. Or you may not remember what pictures were hanging on the walls or what conversations you had with your brothers or sisters.

Whenever you write about a setting, you will engage in some filtering, the same way your memory does. When working from memory, you will probably spend considerable time trying to retrieve as much information about that time and place as possible. When working in the present, the scene is right in front of you, yet you must still be selective about what to include. If, when working from memory, you remain as true to the original experience as possible, then you might call what you produce memoir, a form of nonfiction, which we will discuss more in a coming chapter. You might also include very accurate and detailed memories in a poem. If, however, you start with memory and take some liberties, then you will likely call it fiction, if it is prose. Poetry or drama can also take considerable license with the past.

Similarly, when we write we may combine images that we remember from the same place but from slightly different times. Or we may know that a series of events happened in a place over a period of time, but when remembering it, we put them all together as if they happened at the same time or in a shorter period of time. When writers do this deliberately, it is called *telescoping*, and it can often be an effective technique to heighten the tensions in a narrative.

Memory often plays these kinds of tricks with reality. Have you ever "remembered" something from when you were two or three? Some people have these early memories, and they may indeed be real. Others have memories of something they did at this age, not because they remember it, but because they have been told a story about it so many times. Similarly, we may remember an event or a place where we never could have been, the memory constructed out of other people's experience that has become internalized. Or we simply misremember the details of an experience, yet the misinformation is so ingrained in our heads that we insist we are correct, even if presented with evidence to the contrary. How many sibling arguments occur for this very reason?

Memory can be slippery. It comes and goes, it leaves out important details and fishes up an image that may seem insignificant or that only takes on significance because it has been isolated in the memory. We wonder why this is what we remember. Memory skips around in time and leaves enormous gaps. Though these gaps might be retrieved with thoughtful reflection, some writers rely on the gaps in the story to present a reality that is true to memory, not to the way things actually happened. Imagine writing the story of a person suffering from Alzheimer's, where remembered reality invades present reality to the extent that times, places, and people overlap. Viewed from the outside, the experience must be utterly confusing and frustrating. For the character, that reality may seem utterly seamless and coherent, even if it doesn't match the external world around them. Writers can use memory or the perception of reality to gain a different perspective.

Even if your attempt is to remain relatively true to an actual remembered experience, it is likely you will have to fill in some of the gaps with invention. You may remember that there were pictures and even the kind of pictures they were, but you may not remember them exactly. If it is important to include them at all, you would have license to make up a description that fits the emotional reality of the experience. You wouldn't add something that would feel out of place (without good reason), but you might include a detail that could have been there, but that you don't actually remember. Taking some license with the past is legitimate, even in memoir. How much license you take and how true you remain to the experience is a personal decision, though it might affect what you decide to call your writing.

Take this idea a little further, and it becomes clear that you don't have to stick with memory or write only about what actually happened. You may remember the town where you grew up or a place that you visited once. If your memory is clear enough, this may provide the setting, but you might populate that setting with characters that may be like the people you actually knew there or may be complete fabrications. You might put yourself in a setting, but make your character take more risks than you would have taken. You can play the game of "what if?" What if a crime had been committed and you or your friends witnessed it—how might you have responded? What if you were 5 or 10 years older? What if you were the criminal or knew the criminal? Of course, it doesn't have to be a crime. It could be any act that might have changed, however slightly, the course of your personal history. What if you had gotten up the nerve to go out on that first date? What if you had stayed home instead?

In fiction, poetry, or drama, writers can explore many alternate realities. Memory may provide the fodder, but the fertile imagination can take it anywhere. The same is true for lived experience, of course. There is no law that says writers can't bend or change the truth of what they see, as long as they can justify it (or get away with it). We simply call it *poetic license*.

Whether inspired by the present reality or by memories of the past, most artists will take some liberties with reality to meet the demands of their medium. A painter must alter the actual proportions of things to create a sense of perspective, for instance. A writer is no different.

Though the goal may be an accurate portrayal of reality, it remains a portrayal and as such must bend or even change reality to give the illusion of reality.

Research

So far in this chapter and in the previous one, we have confined our discussion primarily to the experience of the writer, whether that experience is in the present or the remembered past. It's not a bad place to start, and often beginning writers are given the good advice to "Write what you know." Certainly, it can save a lot of headaches or embarrassment to know what you're writing about, and lived experience likely has the most emotional truth for a writer. Goodness knows, when you're starting out, there are so many other craft issues to be concerned with that it may help to begin on familiar ground. And yet, even then, you may find you need to expand on your own experience somewhat.

Let's say you do want to write about your childhood. Where does it say that you can only write about yourself? You may decide that you'd rather invent a character, or you'd rather write your mother's story instead of your own. How do you know what she felt or experienced? You were there, so you may have some idea, but you also were concerned about your own issues and likely were oblivious to hers more or less, depending on your age at the time. Of course, you're able to take license and invent her reality, but you may want more to go on than your imagination.

Writers rarely make things up out of whole cloth, though that is a possibility. Often a writer will spend time in research, filling in the gaps of what they know. This may mean the kind of library or internet research with which you are already familiar: finding street names or tracking down the date of an event, confirming what songs were playing on the radio in a given month of a given year, or any of a million other details that you might want to know but can't remember with confidence.

Still there are other kinds of research that can be equally important. Writers of historical fiction often argue that it is better to read in a period than about it, for instance. Rather than looking up facts that you know you should know from a year that you want to write about, you might spend time reading newspapers or magazines from that year. It may be that the articles themselves provide the information you're looking for, but it may also be that the seemingly insignificant things—the ads, letters to the editor, public notices, etc.—provide the most useful insight into the world of that time and place. What words did people use? What was their slang? What kinds of appliances or cars or clothes were in style?

Newspapers, magazines, and other documents can provide inspiration for new work, whether that is a found poem that reorganizes a paragraph into lines to highlight certain words or images or whether it is a story, essay, or play based more or less loosely on an actual event. Research may be finding the story itself, and the rest may be filled in by imagination, especially with fiction. Or research may begin with finding the story and continue with filling in the gaps and discovering the story behind the story through interviews, further reading, collecting evidence, etc. Many writers move beyond their own experience inspired by real past events, though they may attempt to accurately portray them or they may make no bones about inventing a fiction.

Perhaps better than (or at least as helpful as) book learning may be talking to other people who went through that time. If you want to write about your childhood, consider interviewing your family or your friends to get their perspectives. Collect oral histories or conduct those inter- views yourself. Watch old movies or TV shows (but remember they are only one window on reality). Go to the places you want to write about, if you can, and see what they are like today. Ask the locals about the past or visit a local archive to look at pictures. Attempt to do the things that your characters or the speakers of your poems do. You may learn more by doing than by reading about a way of life.

If you can't go back in time and live like your characters lived, then try to get a better sense of the time through visual representations. Photographs can often be a huge inspiration for the writer, both for the subject of the photograph and for the details that can be found in the background. Like memory that is fragmentary at best, the photograph suggests as much by what it leaves out as by what it includes within its frame. Many a writer begins with the details in the picture and imagines the life the subject must have led outside its boundaries or imagines the thoughts that are going on in the subject's head.

Photographs, paintings, drawings, music, pottery, jewelry, or artwork can do much to evoke the time and place where they were created or used as well as the artist's unique vision of that time and place. The technical term for writing about another work of art is *ekphrasis*. This ancient Greek word originally meant a vivid description of a thing, but now is usually limited to a poem or other writing about a work of art, which typically is a visual artwork. Generally it does more than describe the work of art; it comments on it or extends it. The work of art inspires the writer, not to copy but to respond.

Tradition

While the writer may be inspired by other art forms, and it is excellent advice to visit a museum or attend a concert looking for inspiration, another form of inspiration comes from literature itself. In the introduction, we discussed reading as part of the writing process. Reading to learn how other writers have attained the effects in their work is one part of that process.

Understanding the literary traditions in which you want to write is another important step in the training of any writer. Certainly no writer has read everything that has ever been written, especially not since the twentieth century when the sheer volume of past writing has grown to enormous proportions. The number of recent writers is overwhelming, let alone the number of past writers, now that the world of literature has opened itself through translation and inclusivity to more classes, genders, and cultural traditions.

Though the vast number of works in the literary canon may boggle the mind, it also presents the writer with a multitude of traditions from which to choose. It may be impossible to know it all, but it is not impossible to be well versed in mainstream literature and to explore the urban alleyways or country roads that most strike your fancy. To a certain degree, a writer today can choose her or his own tradition, though most of us will also be informed by our education. We will share certain seminal works with others in our generation, and we will strike out on our own to discover new influences.

Consider the writers or poets and storytellers who have already influenced your sense of story. It is quite likely that as a child you read or were told folk tales or fairy tales. If not, your sense of story may be more informed by classic children's literature or by urban legend. Whatever your background, there is still ample time to explore another area. Are you fascinated by the lives of the Greek, Norse, or African gods and goddesses? Are you interested in folk tales from around the world or would you prefer to read Icelandic sagas or Arthurian romances?

Whatever your interests, these literary traditions may provide a world and even characters to write about. Many poets have taken on classic folk tale characters like Cinderella or Little Red Riding Hood and the Wolf. They may retell the story with a modern twist or they may tell it from a different character's perspective. Some have said there are no new stories under the sun, only new variations to write them down in.

Besides mining a tradition for images, settings, or characters, many writers rely on a tradition to develop a sense of form. A folk tale often follows a recognizable pattern. A ballad will likely deal with one of several themes: love, war, death, or possibly all of the above. Knowing the patterns that a certain kind of story, poem, or play usually follows helps the writer to decide whether to hold to those patterns or to surprise the reader with new variations.

Since we are talking about recognizable patterns in writing, this is a good place to revisit the issue of *genre*. Typically in this book, I have and will use the term genre to refer to the "big" types of writing: drama, nonfiction, poetry, or fiction. Yet within fiction there is a more specific use of the term. *Genre fiction* usually refers to a work of fiction that remains faithful to the established conventions of a tradition. Romance writers are well-known for following certain rules. Mystery writers may have somewhat more flexibility, yet the crime is almost always solved, usually by the detective, though sometimes by an amateur or another party. Westerns typically end with the hero riding off into the sunset, though there are acceptable alternate endings. Science fiction has its conventions of what laws of physics can be broken (how often have we heard of "warp speed" in science fiction, yet science persists with the theory of relativity that states that objects cannot travel faster than the speed of light?).

Though there is nothing inherently wrong with genre fiction, it does present some issues in an introductory creative writing textbook. The greatest of these is that genre fiction relies heavily on established conventions, and in a short book like this, it would be impossible to teach all of those conventions. Even though genre fiction uses conventions, it also relies on many of the techniques of good fiction: clear writing, vivid descriptions of setting, convincing characters, and plots that develop and ultimately resolve tensions, to name a few. Working on those basics now will help a writer who wants to enter the world of genre fiction later. For this reason, some creative writing instructors restrict students in an introductory class from writing genre fiction; others are open to writing on subjects associated with a genre, even if they may not attempt to cover all of the conventions of these genres.

One definition of genre fiction is that it is fiction that follows the rules of an established genre, whereas literary fiction is fiction that creates its own rules to fit the needs of the story. A detective story that reinvents the rules of mystery writing is, by this definition, literary. Though your instructor probably won't ask you to completely reinvent a genre if you want to write about a subject that might fit in a genre like mystery or science fiction, she or he may ask you to consider the demands of the story first, rather than the demands of the genre. Whether or not your instructor allows certain subjects, she or he will ask for your best writing, in other words.

✒ Writing Journal Exercises

1. In a few paragraphs, relate a family story or memory. First write a paragraph or two the way you would write it down, then try to tell it the way someone else in the story might tell it. If possible, interview that person before you try to write their version of the story.
2. In a paragraph or two, describe a place where you used to go when you were about 10 years old. Try to be as specific as possible about the things you remember in that place. Focus on the images that hold the strongest emotional attachment for you. You don't have to describe what the attachment is, just write about those images.
3. Go to the art museum on your campus or to a local museum or gallery. Write about one of the works of art on display. You may begin by describing something in the art, then write about something outside the artwork. You might write about what you imagine just beyond

the frame of the picture, or you might write about what the subject is thinking (if it is not human, use personification). Or you might write about what you imagine the artist felt or experienced. Or you might write about someone who views the work of art: either yourself or another person (real or imagined) who sees it.

4. Visit your local library and look in their archives for pictures of the town or campus from a year before you were born. Write about the place you discover there and compare it to the place you inhabit now. Write about the people in the pictures or the people you imagine living in that place at that time. What would it have been like to live there then?

5. Stop at a historical marker and read the description of whatever event it chronicles. Write a description of the place where the marker stands, both now and during the events that are described on the marker. Try to capture a feeling of both times in your passage. Don't worry yet whether it is a story or a poem, but concentrate on the concrete, physical impressions of the place in two times. If there are people, feel free to include them.

6. Write down the first five or more things you did yesterday morning. Now write five different actions you did yesterday, five or more sounds you heard yesterday, five or more smells (scents, fragrances, whatever) you smelled yesterday, five or more tastes—try to include one taste that isn't food, five or more textures or other feelings such as the temperature, five or more movements you saw other people or things doing. Now pick any three or more of those recent memories involving different senses, and describe them in more detail.

7. Go through a family photo album and look for interesting pictures, whether you are in them or not. Write a paragraph or two about the most interesting one or ones. You might elaborate on what was going on in the picture or you might write about something else that happened at the time the picture reminds you of. Or you might write about one of the people in the picture and your memories of that person.

8. Find some old magazines or newspapers. Look at the ads or the letters to the editor or the advice columns. Try to get a sense of how people talked and the things that were new or important to them at the time.

Write a description of something you found in one of the pictures or write a letter to someone of that time, telling them how much things have changed.

9. Rewrite a folk tale or other familiar story in a new time. Transport an urban legend to the distant past or a myth or legend to a contemporary setting. Begin it as a poem or story with concrete detail. Combine elements of the original with details from the new time and place.

6

Invented Worlds

Dreams

So far, we have mostly discussed creative writing as if the only option were realism. When discussing memory in the previous chapter, we began to branch out with the idea that memory can bend or reshape the reality we lived through, telescoping time or combining memories, even inventing memories. Yet the primary basis for this material came from and was judged against the real world to a greater or lesser degree. Realism isn't the only option a writer has, though.

With enough imagination, the written word can take us places that don't or even can't exist. One model for this kind of invention can come from the world of dreams.

Dreams are familiar. Everyone has them, though some remember their dreams more than others. We all know more or less how dreams operate. They seem real while we are in them, yet we know they are not. Sometimes we even realize we are dreaming while we are still in the dream, yet the experience of the dream still is vivid.

Dreams operate on their own kind of logic. They defy the rational logic of the waking world and instead follow an irrational, associative logic that only makes sense within the context of the dream. You may be talking to one person one minute in a dream and then suddenly realize it is someone else. You may walk out of your house in the dream and end up, not in your front yard, but beside a castle or a waterfall. The familiar and the fantastical are often combined in seemingly endless patterns until the dream plays out or the dreamer awakes.

Some theorists suggest that all of literature operates this way, that a story or poem is a linguistic game that invents its own rules as it goes along. There is nothing about a story that inherently demands that it must conform to reality, in other words. If the story creates a reality where a character can change shape, then the fact that in real life humans don't do this doesn't stop the characters. Look at ancient myth. There, gods and goddesses, heroes and heroines, accomplished feats no ordinary mortal could. Yet the stories told in myth or in folklore resonate with the people who tell them in the same way that dreams do.

When we have a striking dream, we often try to uncover its meaning, as if our subconscious mind is trying to speak to us. Psychologists Sigmund Freud and Carl Jung theorized on the interpretation of dreams. Whether to buy their theories or not is up to you, but the fact that the theories exist goes to show that humans ascribe meaning to dreams, whether that is a revelation of prophecy or deep insight into the psyche of the dreamer.

Writers can learn a lot from studying dreams, though you don't have to study psychology to do so. Record your own dreams and you may find that you remember more of them. The best time to write down a dream is right after you have dreamt it, either in the morning or when you wake in the middle of the night. Many writers who want to be inspired by their dreams keep a notepad at their bedside so they can write them down as soon as possible. Others train themselves to remember their dreams in the morning, by writing them down shortly after they wake. Even if you don't write down every dream, though, there are probably dreams that you can remember even years after the fact. Often these are recurring dreams or nightmares that have revisited you over and over.

Consider what happens in your dreams. What images, actions, or characters reappear in different forms? What shapes, colors, or other qualities do they have in common? Often the seemingly random shifts in images share some common quality, though it may not always be visual and it may not be easy to pin down. We sense that there is a logic to the dream, even though there can be abrupt shifts in time and place. A story or poem based on dreams can use the same kind of associative logic, though it can be a challenge to try to be illogical. Dreams work the way they do because that is the way our subconscious minds work, at least in theory. It can be challenging, but not impossible, for the conscious mind to mimic that without coming across as fake.

Surrealism

For centuries, writers and other artists have let their imaginations run wild and explored images, characters, and worlds that cannot exist in reality. One of the most sustained literary efforts to explore the world of the subconscious mind was made by the Surrealists, a group of writers and artists who started out in Paris in the 1920s. Their self-proclaimed leader was the poet André Breton, who wrote three surrealist manifestoes, laying out the goals of the group and including fellow writers or kicking them out of the movement if they did not subscribe to his artistic and political agenda.

Breton had served in World War I as an army psychologist, treating soldiers with shell shock. It was there that he became interested in their dreams and began to read the early works of Freud and Jung. Surrealism began as an attempt to record the workings of the subconscious mind, not necessarily as a literary experiment. As he noted in the first Surrealist Manifesto, Breton wanted to record pure "psychic automatism" in the absence of any conscious, moral, or esthetic control.

To do this, he developed the technique of *automatic writing*. Essentially, the Surrealists would clear their mind of any thought, put their pen to paper and write whatever words came to mind in free association. Often the resulting text was somewhat grammatical, but the words did not make any kind of logical sense. When the writer realized he or she was consciously thinking about what to say next, the idea was to start the next word with a letter chosen at the outset. Since these were meant to be experiments in recording the subconscious mind, not great poems, it is likely that many made no sense whatsoever. However, through this process Breton discovered striking combinations of images that were suggestive, even provocative.

Other experiments began with collaborative exercises such as *cadavre exquis* (or exquisite corpse), named after a pair of words that resulted from one of the experiments. In this exercise, several people would work together. A paper was divided into parts of speech, so the resulting combination would form a sentence with noun, verb, object, adjective, etc. The paper was folded back after each person wrote a word, so the next person would only see what part of speech he or she had to write, but would not see the words that came before. Striking, if somewhat random, word combinations were discovered through this process.

In many ways Surrealism reminds us that the basis of all writing is in language. Surrealism is formed through word play, and often the word associations are not formed through meaning, but through the sound of the word or through shared qualities in the images. As in free association, one word calls forth another, not because of a rational connection but because of subtle connotations. The surrealist isn't trying to communicate a predetermined message, but instead seeks to discover new meanings through language and image.

One famous early description of surrealism is "the chance encounter of a sewing machine and an umbrella on a dissecting table." Through these strange combinations, the Surrealists hoped to discover the marvelous, rather than the beautiful. They sought to explore the connections between the dream and reality and to enter a heightened reality (*sur* means above in French).

Because they disavowed any moral censure and reveled in breaking taboos, and because they were influenced by Freudian and Jungian psychology, their work is often highly sexualized and in the 1920s was scandalous. Of course, if you think about it, dreams can make you blush too, and some dreams you would only tell to your analyst (if you had one) or your closest friend.

Of course, the Surrealists were not the first to explore this kind of altered reality, and indeed many of them had come from other Modernist literary movements before they coalesced around these ideas. The term *surreal* itself was coined by the cubist poet Guillaume Apollinaire, whose experiments were certainly an inspiration to the Surrealists. Unfortunately, Apollinaire died in the Spanish flu epidemic at the end of World War I while he was recovering from a head wound. Other poets, including

André Breton, had been part of the Dada movement that started in Zurich during the war and moved to Paris afterwards.

Dada, like Surrealism, was based on random associations of words, but Dada was more random than even Surrealism. One famous description of the Dada method, written perhaps tongue-in-cheek by Tristan Tzara, involved cutting up a newspaper article into individual words, tossing the words into a hat, then pulling them out one by one and writing them down in whatever order they appeared. Hugo Ball wrote sound poems composed of vowels and consonants that do not form any recognizable words in any language. The Dada poet explored nonsense and used it as an objection against a European culture that was destroying itself in a world war, but the goal was to challenge our notions of sense, not to make any sense.

The Surrealists, on the other hand, attempted to create a new kind of sense using similar techniques, but believing that the seemingly random associations would in fact be informed by the subconscious to form a new kind of sense. Surrealist poems can still be incredibly frustrating to read if you are looking for a clear idea of their meaning. If you are willing to give in to the flow of images and let meaning accumulate intuitively, they can be fascinating, unconventional, even beautiful.

The early experiments in automatic writing and collaborative writing would eventually give way to somewhat more controlled attempts at poetry that worked with similar associative images.

Pure automatic writing does not allow for any revision, in other words. The only way to "improve" is with practice, and the only judge of improvement would be how little conscious control was exerted in the process. The poet Robert Desnos was famous for going into a self-hypnotic trance at the drop of a hat and speaking oracular phrases or answering questions with cryptic answers. André Breton would publish some of his own early automatic writing as the book of prose poems *Poisson Soluble* (*Soluble Fish*). Later books of poems were written in lines, rather than prose, but retained the free association of images. Surrealism spread beyond Paris to other European cities and even New York. It has remained an important influence on poetry throughout the twentieth and into the twenty-first century.

Surrealism did not only affect poetry, of course. It has been a major movement in the visual arts and even in early cinema. The Surrealists wrote novels as well as poems, and one could argue that it was a major influence on the Magical Realist movement as well. Magical Realism combines elements of dream and folklore with realism to create fictions that are part tall tale, part fable, and part political or social commentary. Postmodern fiction, with its emphasis on the fact that the story is a story, not a real event, is also arguably influenced by Surrealism.

Alternate Realities

Of course, Surrealism is not the only alternative to realism. Besides the recent literary movements just mentioned, many literary forms have created alternate realities. Still, Surrealism can be instructive. Though Surrealism creates a new reality, it doesn't create it out of thin air.

Surrealism, like dreams, relies on images found in the real world. It transforms them and recombines them to create fantastical realms, and it breaks the laws of physics, but it does not abandon them completely. Always, reality is a part of surreality, even if it is only an echo, and the surreal experience is most interesting when it sheds light on the real, in the same way that the dream is typically more memorable when we sense some connection to waking life.

So, too, with fantasy or science fiction. When writers in these genres create their worlds, they operate on rules that are reflections of our own. Wizards or elves may use magic, yet there are limits to what they can do. Though beings in these worlds may be more powerful than mortals, they still operate within some kind of morality, or if a world is described as completely amoral, it is recognizably so in contrast to our own.

The characters in these stories may face challenges that could never be faced in the real world, yet their choices parallel our own. When the fantasy or the science of these fictions overwhelms the human element, many readers will lose interest. Similarly, plot alone can rarely drive a story. This is not to say that the imagined worlds must be similar to our own, only that they need to be somehow connected to ours. A story may take place on a planet light years away from earth with alien creatures that bear no physical likeness to humans, and yet if we can see ourselves reflected in their world, however distorted that reflection may be, then there is interest. A fairy realm or a world where magic, vampires, zombies, or gods exist may be interesting in its own right, but it will hold our interest best if we can relate to their trials and concerns.

Maintaining Tensions

When describing any world, one issue is to keep the description lively and interesting. Whether your world is the real world around you, a remembered world, or one invented through imagination, if the images you present of it are one-sided, the description can soon become monotonous. Perhaps with invented worlds, the challenge is greater, since you don't have the real world before you with all its endless variety. When we invent a world, we see what we want to see, and we may have to work harder to envision the complexities needed for a full portrayal. Yet if we stick to one kind of image, a descriptive passage can feel flat and even action can become dull if it is too repetitive, if there are no ups and downs, no suspense.

A scene of a perfect, sunny day can quickly become tedious if nothing threatens that perfection. In the same way, a scene of violence and death can become overwhelming or even gratuitous if it goes on for too long with no interruption or sense of something better. The love poem with no potential heartache may easily turn saccharine sweet, and the poem of religious devotion may be hard to believe if there is no sense of doubt.

Good writing lives and breathes on contrasts and tensions: not necessarily conflict, though often tension is seen and even portrayed in those terms. Conflict occurs when characters actively are at odds with one another. Tension happens when they know they are at odds, but haven't acted on it yet, and may decide not to. Conflict is overt action; tension can be subtly conveyed through many details, even if no characters are present.

Consider a photograph taken on a cloudy day. The light in the picture tends to be washed out and everything is fairly monotone. Without good lighting, it's hard to take a good photo because there is no contrast to add definition to the people or objects within the frame. On the other hand, a bright, sunny day at noontime often is a challenge for the opposite reason.

The contrasts are too extreme: everything is light or shadow, and there are no midtones. Finding or creating good lighting means choosing the location or setting up your flash so that the angle of the light highlights the subject in interesting ways that keep the viewer's eyes engaged in the image.

Writers face a similar challenge, to find the angle of vision that presents the right level and the right kind of contrast in the world they portray. Too little contrast, a focus on one quality of that world, and the reader quickly loses interest; too much contrast, extreme shifts or a very dualistic portrayal, runs the risk of driving away the reader as well. Somewhere in between these extremes, in the range of many possible levels of contrast, lies the option that best highlights your subject. In a poem this may mean bringing in a few light images to contrast with the darker ones, using sad thoughts to counterbalance the happy tone, or finding lighter sounds to contrast with the heavier ones. In a story there may be evil to counter the good. Or you might prefer to think in terms of the not-so-bad versus the not-so-good. Or perhaps everyone in the story is good enough (no value judgments), but their interests and goals are different enough that they contrast with each other.

When writing, try to explore your world in rich detail and in all of its complexity. This will almost guarantee some contrast and some tension, which you may want to organize and highlight in more specific ways in revision. When revising your writing, pay particular attention to the general tone of the piece, then look to see whether you have written both (or all) sides to the picture.

If a passage starts to lose interest and seems to drag on and not lead anywhere, don't feel bad. It's quite likely you've painted one side of the picture and you need to bring in some of the other side for contrast. That doesn't mean all of the writing you have done for that passage is no good, only that it needs contrast and tension to bring out the good. But do be prepared. Adding contrast and tension, even conflict, can often change a poem or scene and take it in new and unexpected directions. Be willing to follow your intuition and let the tensions play out.

The story that began as the perfect romance may need a level of mistrust and jealousy to give it tension and keep the energy going. The happy couple may move beyond their fears, and the temptress (or tempter) may not win the heart of the hero (or heroine). The couple may end up together after all. But you may find that it feels more true to life to allow jealousy to ruin the relationship, for the heartless love who seemed so perfect in the beginning to leave his or her partner in the lurch, following some ill-fated new romantic quest, while the reader is left to sympathize with the jilted lover.

There are many permutations of this storyline, and any could seem realistic, depending on how you tell it. The point is not that the story of love lost is better than the story of love found.

Rather, my point is that introducing contrast, tension, and even conflict into your writing, whether that is through action or description, is more than adding highlights or shadows to round out the picture that is already painted. Adding tension introduces a new dynamic to the piece. It adds a level of uncertainty for the writer, and ultimately for the reader. If the story or poem could go either way (or in one of several directions), you hold our interest.

For many writers, writing is a process of discovery. Whether in a poem, story, play, or essay, the writer sets up different contrasting elements: images, characters, ideas, etc. The writer sets them loose on the stage of the imagination, on the blank page of the unwritten piece, and gradually works toward a resolution of these opposites. When it becomes too easy, the writer introduces new tensions to mess things up and keep it interesting, until the conclusion (whether a resolution of all the tensions or only some of them) feels satisfying. Some writers want to know the end before they begin, so they can find the best way there. But many writers only want to start somewhere in the middle of the action and work their way to an uncertain ending. Either strategy can work as long as there are enough tensions and enough uncertainty along the way to hold the reader's interest. Finding those tensions and exploring the issues they raise is part of the challenge and part of the fun for most writers.

◗ Writing Journal Exercises

1. Record one of your dreams. Try to be as detailed in your memory as possible, but don't embellish. It is best to try recording your dream when you first wake up or to keep your journal by your bedside so you can

62   A Writer's Craft

write in the middle of the night, if you need to. After you have recorded the dream as you dreamt it, you may want to pull out images or even the narrative for a story or poem. You might start this outside your journal on a pad or piece of paper you keep near your bed, especially if you're not sure you want to share all of the details. Copy it into the journal later.

2. Imagine a situation like a storm or an accident or a wedding or a beach vacation, etc. List all the positive aspects of that situation, then make a separate list of all the negative aspects. Which things about that situation could be included in both lists? Write a scene incorporating elements of both lists. Try to draw on some of the elements you thought could be both positive and negative and bring out their dual quality.

3. Try automatic writing. Write for at least a minute without stopping to think about what you will write. Start with a quiet room. Clear your mind of any conscious thought. Then put your pen to paper and write the first words that come to mind. Try not to think about what word will come next, and allow the sentences to make their own kind of sense or nonsense. If you find that you are thinking about what to write, begin the next word with the letter p. Don't take your pen from the page and don't stop writing until you have filled at least half of a page.

4. Describe the world from an unusual perspective. You might describe a room as it would look from a spider's point of view or describe a town from an outsider's perspective. Consider what a city looks like from the water tower or to a sewer rat. Write about the inside of something you usually perceive from the outside.

5. Find a text that strikes you for one reason or another, where the language is unusual or so normal that it's interesting. Your text can come from an ad, a product description, a newspaper story, etc. Copy the most interesting sentences into your journal verbatim. Don't worry about whether they are poetic. You are simply collecting language at this point. Then rewrite the whole quote, using antonyms for the important words. Revise this as a poem or paragraph, selecting the most interesting phrases, cutting out or changing the less interesting ones. Concentrate on the sound as well as the meaning of the words as you revise.

6. Take an ordinary, everyday object or situation and describe it as if you were seeing it for the very first time. Perhaps you are a foreigner or an alien who has never encountered it. Describe it in detail, but look for

the details that you normally would overlook. Question the use of this object or the point of the situation. If you didn't know the answer, what might you guess this object or situation could be?

7. Imagine you are a time traveler from the distant future or past and you have landed in your actual home town. You have no idea when or where you are. What are some of the first details you would notice that would give you a clue that you aren't where you thought you were? Describe those details from this unfamiliar perspective. What would you think of our streets, our clothes, our advertisements, or the way people walk, talk, and interact with each other? Concentrate on the small details that would seem utterly strange to someone who was unfamiliar with them.

8. Write a sentence or two on any topic. Then look up each noun and verb in your sentence, preferably in a print dictionary. Find the seventh entry after the word in your sentence and write it above your word. Copy your passage, replacing the words with their counterpart seven entries later in the dictionary. Continue the new passage for another sentence or more in the same vein by writing about the new "surreal subject" using random or associative shifts in language and imagery.

7

Character and Voice

Character

In the previous three chapters, our discussion of writing has primarily focused on place: where you go for inspiration. Writers may draw on their experience of the world around them, they may draw on memory, or they may draw on their dreams and imagination, yet for many writers this may not be enough or it may not be where they go first. Often, writers say that a story or poem begins, not with the plot or with the setting, but with a character. Once the writer knows who he or she is going to write about, then the other things begin to fall into place. Other writers start with a place and only then begin to populate it with one or more characters. And occasionally a writer will know what is going to happen before knowing where and to whom it will happen. As with so many issues in writing, there is no one right way to do it. There is no right order to write in. But one thing is true: whether the characters emerge first or whether they emerge later in the process, compelling characters are essential to most good writing.

Naturally, we expect characters in fiction and drama. We also expect them in some forms of nonfiction, such as in autobiography or docudrama. We may not expect them as much in the personal essay or in a poem, where the use of character is often much more subtle and minimal.

Perhaps there is only a word or an image that gets at the character in a poem or even in flash fiction. Yet often, if not always, the writing arises out of a sense of character, even if the character is a persona of the writer. When the voice of a poem seems forced or contrived, the reader may feel preached at or the poem may lack credibility. When plot seems to dictate character or to contradict or ignore the characters, then the story begins to feel arbitrary and forced. That's not to say that an arbitrary plot that emphasizes the fact that it is a created fiction can't be written—it has been by many postmodern writers—but since it runs counter to readers' expectations, such a plot is even trickier to manage well than a realist one. Typically characters and the actions they take or the things they say are meant to seem real and natural.

Yet what do we mean when we talk about real or natural characters? On the one hand, it may seem like the most obvious thing in the world, and on the other hand, you may be wondering, where do I begin? In realist fiction, as in most other writing, readers expect *well-rounded characters*. We expect complex characters that look, think, and act like real people. That seems obvious, but how do you get that illusion to happen in the reader's mind when all you have to work with are words on a page? In a way, this is a lot like the challenge of taking plain, bland description and transforming it into an image that elicits an emotional response from a reader. There seems to be a bit of magic involved, but fortunately we can break it down enough to at least get you started, so that maybe the magic, the spark of imagination, will catch fire.

If you think about it, our first impressions of a literary character are pretty similar to our first impressions of a person. When people talk about "love at first sight," we assume that a relationship has begun from physical attraction. Sometimes it is simply because the other person is exceptionally beautiful (and we wonder if the "love" will last), but other times the attraction is harder to define and stems from subtle cues that we pick up on: a smile, the look in the other person's eyes, the way they dress, or the way they walk across a room. Something about that person grabs our attention and we are hooked.

In the same way, physical description can reveal a lot about a character. Physical description can be both the way characters look and the look characters choose to present to the world: their physical features, the clothes they wear and how they wear them, their hair color and style, etc. Physical description can also include what Tim O'Brian called "the things they carry," the props and possessions associated with the character. Even the world the character inhabits can be a reflection of who they are as a person. A story may include elaborate descriptions of the characters in the beginning to orient the reader, or a story may give only subtle hints now and then, the flashes of insight that often catch our eye.

Often before even beginning a story, a writer lists these kinds of details to write a *character sketch*. You may begin with a name or you may begin with a description. How much does a name tell about a character? Does the character live up to his or her name or does he or she struggle against it? How old is the character and where does he live or what kind of car does she drive? Many writers will begin with long lists of everything they can imagine about the character in the present and in the past. Moving beyond physical images, the writer might fill in the blanks of education and career, family and friends.

As you move beyond the initial physical description, you begin to get to know your character better. The more you know about your characters, the more you are able to predict how they might react in a given situation. A story may even begin to develop as you discover the other people this character interacts with on a daily basis. Does she have siblings? Has she met someone at work? Did he run into a stranger on the street, in a coffee house, at a sporting event? What might happen as a result of this encounter?

Motivation

When an actor prepares to play a character in a play, she often has to do more than memorize her lines. She has to know not only what the character says, but why she says it, and how she walks, moves, sits, gestures, etc. Many actors imagine a complete life for their character. They spend a lot of time studying the script for clues, but they also make up a life for the character that fits the script. An actor needs to know what happened to the character right before he or she comes on stage, but also what the character is trying to get out of the scene, which is informed by the broader picture of what they really want out of life. In other words, the actor invents a life for her character so that she knows the character's *motivation*, the desires and goals that drive the scene and may make a difference to the speed at which she walks across a room or the inflection that she gives a line of dialogue.

Writers often do the same thing when they write a character sketch. You want to explore the characters' lives in a character sketch, so you know what motivates them in the story and you know how they will respond in different situations. Some writers could tell you exactly why their characters act the way they act, possibly from some deep psychological desire or possibly from a more direct physical need like hunger. Often, writers know much more about their characters than they can ever include in a story, but they know it so they can choose what to include and how their characters will interact with one another. Other writers make only limited notes about their characters and don't try to psychoanalyze them, but instead rely on their own intuition to know how a character will act. Many authors have said that they wanted a character to have a different choice in the end, but they knew that the character had to make the wrong choice because it felt right. In other words, there is a certain level of consistency to the character that demands a certain action. Some authors even act as if their characters talk to them, which I take to mean that they have so internalized their characters that they dream about them or think of them as if they were real.

Yet, though there should be consistency, readers of realist fiction expect characters whose lives and choices are complicated, even contradictory. The heroine who is absolutely nice in addition to being beautiful may work in a fairy tale, but she comes across as stale or shallow in a realist story. No one can be that good (and no villain can be absolutely evil, though we may be more willing to accept an evil villain than a saintly protagonist). Every person you know in real life has quirks and contradictions. We say we are going to do one thing, yet turn right around and do another. Or we do what we say, but not for the reasons we want to pretend. Maybe the saint has some self-interest or the great beauty is vain or insecure. In fiction and drama, even poetry or essays, we have come to expect this level of realism. We want to see characters whose desires are complicated and messy, who say one thing, then do another. Maybe it is the villain with an endearing sense of humor or the hero who has to overcome a fear of heights.

All this suggests that, though our initial impressions of a character may stem from the physical description or even their name, the true test of character comes through their actions. We learn more about who people really are from what they do than from what they look like. As readers, we want to suspend our disbelief and think of the characters in a story, play, or poem as real, live people. Too much or too little consistency threatens to break that bubble, so the balancing act is to create a character whose flaws and foibles make him seem real *and* help the reader to understand his actions *and* move the story along (not seem like flaws introduced only to give the character flaws, in other words). This does not mean that writers have to psychoanalyze every character and give (or even have) a rational explanation for every choice that they make. Some writers work this way, but many rely at least in part on their gut. We may not know *why* a character acts the way she does, but we know that a character like her *would* act that way.

How do we know how a character would act? Most writers are keen observers, not only of the world around them, but also of the people in their world. If we weren't, we might not be drawn to creative writing. Some writers base their characters on people they actually know, changing the names and a few details, perhaps, in order to avoid a lawsuit or a family argument. Other writers base their characters not on one person but on a composite of two or more. They may combine character traits of someone they know with the history of someone they have read about, or they may take traits from two or three people they know and combine them to create a character that is similar, yet unlike any of them. Even writers who claim to create characters solely from their imaginations must draw on their experience of people interacting with others.

Well-rounded characters are complicated and believable, whether based on real-life people or made up from the writer's experience and intuition. But not all characters need this level of development. Many stories include *flat characters* that are less developed or based on *stereotypes*. These characters serve their purpose by being instantly recognizable, yet they do not get in the way of the main characters. Think of them like extras on a movie set or bit roles in a play. These characters often recede into the background and are part of the environment that the main character inhabits, but they usually don't advance the story because that is not their role.

Main characters tend to be well rounded and the extras have only enough touches to make them come alive for their brief moment on stage.

Like an actor who plays a bit part, the author may need to imagine the flat character's motivation for one line of dialogue or an action, but the reader may never know anything about the character. All that matters is that the character seems real for that brief moment he or she is part of the story. Some characters start with a cameo appearance in one story but become so intriguing to the writer that they reappear, possibly with a somewhat altered identity, in a bigger role in another story.

After all, characters are not completely well rounded or completely flat, but there is a range of character development in between. While the main characters of a story are generally very well rounded and the extras are extremely flat, receiving only a motion or a few words, there may be other minor roles that receive some development but not as much as the main characters.

Imagine that your character has an aunt who is very important to her. The aunt plays a pivotal role in one scene, but doesn't appear in the rest of your story. Your readers will know much more about the main character than they do about the aunt, yet in preparing for that one scene, you will likely let the readers know enough about the aunt's story so that they can accept whatever role she plays in that pivotal scene. Deciding how much of the character to reveal—and when to reveal it—is part of the writer's task, as is deciding how to reveal character.

Voice

So far, we have discussed character in terms of description and action. Most of what we glean about character, we pick up the way we would in real life, from the little clues we see about them and from the things they do. We judge people primarily by their appearance and their actions.

Another way to reveal character, though, is through *voice*: the way a person talks, as much as the things that a person says, reveals a lot about them.

In real life, of course, we learn a lot about a person from the sound of her voice or from his accent. In drama, an actor can portray this aspect of voice, but in most written texts the reader has to imagine the way the character speaks, and the primary means of getting this across is through *diction*, a combination of word choice and syntax.

If you think about it, besides the kind of accent we speak with, the words that we tend to use tell a lot about who we are. If I have a university education, I am more likely to use ten-dollar words than if I only went to school through the eighth grade. On the other hand, if I am educated but spend much of my time with working-class people, I am likely to talk the way they talk, at least when I am around them. Linguists call this *code switching* and characters may do the same thing: the voice they speak in may change depending on the context. It is not only the words that a character knows that tells us a lot about the character, but the words that character chooses to use in a given context. Someone who uses high-brow language may be trying to impress the person he is talking to. Someone who talks down to another character because he assumes she won't comprehend may come across as haughty or, in this case, even sexist. As we noted in Chapter 3, writers use words on multiple levels. We don't only look for the word with the right meaning; we look for the word that does what we need it to do in a particular context, and often the choice of the right word is determined by character.

If we are writing about a regional character, we may choose to write in *dialect*, though often too much creative spelling can get in the reader's way. Rather than writing in a thick dialect, many writers will choose to hint at a regional pronunciation with a few alternate spellings, but get most of the dialect across by choosing typical words or phrases. Depending on where you live, for instance, you may call a sugary carbonated beverage a "coke," a "soda," or a "pop." When you insert an electrical plug in an outlet, do you say you "plug it up" or "plug it in?" What are some other regional expressions that you know? It's likely, if you have lived all of your life in one area, you may not even recognize what you say differently, though if you make friends with someone from a different region, you'll likely start to notice how they talk. No one is right or wrong. We simply have different colors and flavors of language.

Similar to region, as was suggested above, there are class differences in language. Depending on education, but also depending on how you grew up, you are likely to be more familiar with certain words and even more comfortable with different kinds of sentences. If you speak in fragments or you speak in short declarative sentences, it tells something about you. However, if you tend to use long, complicated sentences with several dependent clauses, then you are likely to reveal something completely different about yourself. Of course, the best way to learn about voice is to listen to the way people talk. And the best way to learn how to approximate this in writing is to read other writers that you admire and pay attention to how they create a voice.

One place in writing where voice is most apparent is in *dialogue*. Like action, dialogue reveals a lot about a character, both through what the character says (or doesn't say) and the way the character says it. Is the character rushed or stressed out? This will show in the way he or she speaks in dialogue. Is the character infuriatingly calm and slow? His or her speech should reflect this. Like all things with character, we tend to expect dialogue to be natural, though in fact it is necessarily artificial.

In real life, our conversations are often mundane and to the point or we beat around the bush endlessly to fill time. We may talk on the phone just for the love of talking or we may have a conversation because we are with someone we haven't seen in a while, but we may not have a specific agenda in mind. In a story, and even more so in a poem, dialogue must accomplish several tasks at once. Obviously, it must work as a speech act within the context to convey information. Yet it also gives subtle cues to the reader about the character. And the information that it conveys or the task that it tries to accomplish also must be important to the story or poem. In other words, we assume that characters say a lot more to one another than is reported in a story, in the same way that they probably brush their teeth two or three times a day, yet we usually don't have to know about it. The dialogue that we get in a story, play, essay, or poem represents the moments that are the most charged, where the most change occurs. And it is probably condensed compared to what would really happen in life. What might take a five-minute conversation in real life might be portrayed with five lines in a story, maybe a scene that lasts a minute or two in a play. Every word counts, and every word counts on multiple levels.

Though the words that characters say to one another in dialogue tell us a lot about who they are, there are other ways a reader learns about a character. At least in some types of fiction, the narrator can also reveal the *thought* of some characters. Here, too, the diction of the character reveals as much as what is said, though the way a character thinks to herself may contrast with the way she speaks in public. The contrast between the inner voice and the public voice may be one revealing aspect of her character.

So far, we have talked about character and voice primarily in terms of fiction, though I have suggested that they can also be important in poetry. One kind of poem where this is very apparent is the *dramatic monologue.* Like a speech in a play, the dramatic monologue poem is written in a character's voice and from his or her perspective. Robert Browning is a well-known practitioner of the form, with poems like "Porphyry's Lover" and "My Last Duchess." Through the speech of a character, he reveals more than the character intends. We as readers read between the lines of the character's monologue and guess his or her secrets. In this kind of poem, establishing a voice is essential to establishing the character.

The dramatic monologue is an extreme form of the *persona poem*, a poem written in the voice of another. Poets are not limited to writing about their own experience any more than fiction writers are, and many have written about historical figures or other characters, often writing from that character's perspective and in his or her voice. A *persona* is simply the outward character or role that you take on. Often we think of persona in its original context of acting a role, becoming like someone else. However, in a more general sense, your persona can also mean the way you present yourself—it doesn't have to be someone else. A persona is a mask or a character that can be close to but not exactly who you are. In all writing, the writer adopts a persona. It may be very close to their true identity or it may be very foreign to it. The student writing an essay probably knows what her conclusion is going to be, yet in the first paragraph she presents a thesis that she intends to prove, as if she hasn't already thought through that proof. It is a stance that we come to expect.

In the same way, the poet writing an autobiographical poem adopts a certain voice and a certain stance toward the subject of the poem. He may take more or less poetic license with that subject to meet the demands of the poem, but his voice will never be exactly the same as it would be in an essay or in an everyday conversation.

When the persona in a poem is not identified, we refer to it as the *speaker of the poem*. Similarly in fiction or nonfiction, the writer adopts an *authorial voice* that is not exactly her own normal speaking voice. It is crafted to fit the demands of form, and it may be unique to the story or essay. A story may have a *narrator*, who is not exactly the author. In any work of literature, there are multiple layers of voice, as we shall see in the following chapter. Learning to orchestrate these many voices is part of the challenge of becoming a writer. Fortunately, most writers begin by relying on their ear and their instinct, as well as on the strategies they have absorbed from their reading. There is no one right way to do it, and it is the kind of thing that improves with time and with revision. Attentive readers in your workshop can help you see where the voice in a story or poem needs improvement. Reading your work aloud can help you decide for yourself.

Writing Journal Exercises

1. Write a letter from a character that you are working on, either in a story or in one of your journal exercises. The letter should be to another character or to you as author. In it, let the character explain why they did something (preferably something slightly embarrassing) the previous day. The character does not have to tell the whole truth about the incident, but should describe it in his or her own voice as much as possible.

2. Write a composite character sketch. Start by thinking of two people that you know. For each, list as many qualities about them as you can remember (write at least 10). These might be physical traits like hair color, or they might be character traits like patience. Try to be as detailed as possible in your lists. Then write a paragraph describing a new character who has some characteristics drawn from both lists. Choose characteristics that will give your new character complexity and yet make the character unique.

3. Write a character sketch of a character from a story you are working on or from one of your journal exercises. Write lists of as many attributes as you can think of: their physical appearance, the sound of their voice, the things they own or wear, the way they act, what they do for a living, their background, education, etc. Give your character a history and list the things you see as their motivation. Try to find contrasts or contradictions as you write your sketch.

4. In one column, write down a list of categories. On your list, include some things that a character might actually have, like a car, and some things that a character might not own, like an insect. Think of a character you might like to write about. In the second column, write down what specific thing from each category the character would be (if he or she were that thing) or what best represents the character. In the third column, write down what from each category the character actually owns (or has in his/her life). And in the last column, write down what from each category the character wants.

5. Play Truth or Dare with one of your characters. Write a series of questions for the character. Which of the questions would the character answer? Would your character really tell the truth? Or would they lie convincingly? If the character was willing to take a dare, what would the character be willing to do to avoid telling the truth? Or would the character take the dare because it is more fun than telling the truth?

6. Observe a person you don't know for 10 minutes or more. Write down as much as you can about that person: what do they look like, what do they wear, how do they move, or what do they say? Then pick three or more character traits and write down what you think it tells about their character. What can you surmise about the person's life from the things you witness? Make up this person's history, based on what you observe.

7. Listen to the people around you and make a list of the idioms and regional language that they use. Collect a list of at least 20 turns of phrase that are new to you or that you have heard all your life but usually don't notice. Try to pick the most distinctive phrases or words that you might give to a character from this place.

8

Perspective and Point of View

Choosing a Perspective

As the idea for a piece of writing begins to develop, one of the first choices is likely to concern the perspective from which the piece is written. This may begin with the choice of main character or it may begin with an early description. Because the initial choice may not be the best, as a piece develops, it can be a good idea to experiment with different perspectives to see which gives it the most energy. Though it can lead to major revisions, often a change in perspective is just what a story needs to make it feel finished. Try writing from different perspectives. At the very least, it will give you insight into your characters and the world they live in. Even if you don't use those exercises in the finished piece, they will inform the writing that you do.

We can start our discussion of perspective in terms of the angle of vision. If you view a plant or animal from far away, chances are you can see all of it (unless parts are obscured by something else), but you can't see a lot of detail. If it is an animal, like a horse running across a pasture, then you see the movement of the horse, and you may see its mane or its tail, but you probably don't notice every marking on it, and you may not be able to tell whether it is sweating or breathing hard. If, on the other hand, you view the same horse up close, you get an entirely different impression.

You may not even notice the tail, but you might see the ripples of its muscles under the skin, or you might see its gums and teeth or the look in its eye. Chances are, if you are close to a horse, the sight of it may not be the only thing you notice. The scent of the saddle or of the horse itself may be overpowering. The feeling of the horse's hair as you are grooming it may be just as important to you.

Similarly, when you describe any scene, you might be looking at it through one lens or another. Often we talk about these in cinematic terms, so we might discuss a panoramic view or a wide-angle shot. Then we might zoom in to a mid-range shot or a close-up. If you're interested in every little detail, you might call it a macro view, based on the term for extreme close-up in photography. Whether these terms speak to you or not, the important thing to remember is that you have options as a writer. You can take any vantage point you need (and you don't need the specialized lenses of the photographer). You can be extremely close to your subject and experience it in every detail and from every sense, or you can be further removed.

You might decide in a poem or essay, for instance, to write from an unusual perspective. Describe the world as if you are standing on your head and everything seems upside down. Or describe your town from the top of a water tower or cell phone tower. It doesn't matter if you've actually been there, as long as you can imagine how it must look. Unique perspectives can lead to new insights about the world or the things in it. They can disorient the reader and allow the reader to see the "normal" world in a whole new light.

Besides the location the story is told from, who tells the story also has a dramatic effect on perspective. If I tell a story from one character's perspective, then there may be some information that I cannot reveal, since that character wouldn't know about it. You might also include some of your character's bias. The details that character would consciously or subconsciously avoid might give the reader some insight into the character's motivations.

Point of View

When you discuss a piece of writing in terms of who is speaking and how the story is told, the technical term for these choices is *point of view*. Typically, we think of point of view primarily for fiction, where it identifies the type of narrator an author uses to relate a story. However, the idea of point of view can be useful to consider in poetry, where we usually talk about a *speaker of the poem*, or even in an essay. In drama the range of points of view is generally more limited, since there typically isn't a narrator, but there are actors that portray the characters. And yet, some of the issues we will discuss with fiction might still apply: how much information about the thoughts of the characters are we given, which character or characters do we follow, etc.?

To begin, then, let us look at the more familiar range of points of view in fiction, where we typically identify three main types: first person, second person, and third person. If you're good at grammar, or if you've studied a foreign language, then you probably know that the first person pronoun is "I." So a first person narrator is one who refers to him or herself using "I." Of course, in reality, it may be an author who takes on a character's voice and tells the story in that persona, using "I" to refer to the character, not the author. Even in autobiography, we might say that the first person narrator isn't exactly the author because every writer takes on a persona when she sits down to write, even if that persona is very close to her true self. Because the narrator is referred to in the text as "I," the narrator becomes a character in the work.

In the other two forms of narration, however, there is no "I." The narrator is not a character, not even a minor one, but the narrator is an unnamed, amorphous figure that tells the story. Many theorists have suggested that the narrator is never exactly the author, though in some works they can be very close. The narrator tells the story; the author creates the narrator who tells the story. And the writer is the person who takes on the persona of author when she sits down to write.

Suddenly, there is a lot of acting and drama in any fiction, and we haven't even gotten to the characters!

Another form of point of view is the second person, which uses a narrator who refers to a "you" or to "we." The narrator himself is not mentioned in the text; he is only the voice that says "you." We know nothing about him, but he (or she) speaks to someone in the second person. The only way the narrator can be included in the text is as part of the general, second person plural, "we." When a narrator speaks to a "you," we generally have three ways to look at it. The story or poem may be addressed to a specific character in the work. A love poem may be addressed to the beloved and only mention the things the narrator loves about him or her. A story may be told by a narrator, speaking to another character and only revealing things about that character and the others around her or him. Another option for the "you" of second person narration is that the writer may be addressing the reader directly. And the third option is that the narrator is using "you" in the less formal, general sense of "one." The sentence, "When you go to the drive-in movie, you pull a little speaker through the window, turn up the volume, eat your popcorn, and ignore the movie," probably isn't talking about any one specific person, but is talking in a general sense about the kinds of things people used to do at a drive-in movie. If there is no "I" in a poem or story, but there is a "you" (no matter how it is used), then we call it second person point of view. It is more common in poetry than in fiction, but it is a possibility for a story, though it can be a challenge to maintain in a long story.

If, on the other hand, the narrator does not use "I" or "you," but only speaks of the characters as "he," "she," or "they," then we call it third person narration. In this case, there is even less information about the narrator. We do not know the relationship of the narrator to the characters. We do not sense the narrator as a character at all, though we may intuit a few things about the narrator from the story that is told and the voice that tells it. We tend to think of the third person narrator as the objective voice of the author, though of course that isn't always the case. A third person narrator can be biased, and a third person narrator may not share the views of the author. An author may hold one view and have the narrator express another view. Through the evidence in the story, the reader might infer the author's view and begin to suspect the statements of the narrator. In this way, *irony* is introduced into a text when the images and actions of the characters contradict the stated views of the narrator. In other words, some authors are tricky, and you may not want to take what their narrator or their characters say at face value. An author may choose a narrator precisely for that reason, to complicate the truths in a text and encourage the reader to figure them out for themselves. A narrator who introduces false information or perspectives, either intentionally or due to limited knowledge or understanding, is considered an *unreliable narrator*.

If point of view were only about pronouns, in other words, then it would be fairly dry and straightforward, and it might not even be worth talking about in this book: just leave it to literary scholars to spend time parsing sentences and dissecting plots. But as I have been trying to suggest, there is a lot more to it than grammar. The choice of a perspective—the personal first person or the more abstract third person, for instance—affects the tone and the very dynamics of a piece of writing. Change perspectives, and you might see a story in a whole new light— what happens if you let one of your characters tell the story in his or her own voice from his or her own perspective? What happens if you remove the "I" from the love poem and focus only on what is desirable about the beloved, not on the desire of the lover? As you are working with early drafts of a poem or story, try out different angles and different points of view until you find the one that works best for you and for the piece. It isn't too hard to go back and revise the scenes or stanzas in a different point of view if you decide you need to do that.

Distance

No matter which pronoun you choose for your narrator to use, another issue you will face with point of view is one of distance. How close is the narrator to the action and to the other characters? How much does the narrator know or how limited is their perspective? Is the narrator reliable or unreliable? There's no right or wrong choice, but each choice makes a difference, and some may be more appropriate for a given story than others would be.

If you choose to write in first person, there are two main options with regard to how close the narrator is to the action. If the narrator is caught up in the main action of the story, if he is the protagonist or the antagonist, then we might call him a *central* first person narrator. If on the other hand, she is on the periphery of the story and only tells what she has seen and heard, then we might call her a *witness* first person narrator. The action does not affect the narrator significantly in this case, or the narrator isn't part of the action, even if it does affect her. Her knowledge of the events in the story is more limited than a central character's would be, and this can be used to good effect.

Consider *The Great Gatsby*. Would Jay Gatsby be as mysterious a character if he told his story himself? Would his love for Daisy be as romantic, if he told it to us? It might come across as sentimental or even pathetic if told in his own words, yet when told by his neighbor Nick Carraway, the reader shares his wonder at the world of Gatsby. We are the outsider looking in, with only some access to their lives. Similarly, the Sherlock Holmes stories are perhaps best told by Watson, who can marvel at Holmes' powers of deduction. If Holmes told the story himself, we might be impatient or feel cheated that he didn't reveal everything he knows before the end of the story. But since we follow Watson's point of view, we are left following the trail of clues as he does, and we have some hope of figuring out the crime before Watson does or before Holmes reveals the solution to him, even though we might never outwit Sherlock himself.

Besides the physical distance from the action, though, a first person narrator may be more or less distant from events in time. A first person story can be told as events are happening, which we might call *immediate* first person narration. Readers are willing to suspend their disbelief and hear a story told by a character in the present tense, as if it is happening right before their eyes as it is told. An extreme form of this would be *stream of consciousness*, where the reader only knows what the narrator perceives and thinks as it happens, but doesn't get any context. James Joyce's *Ulysses* is a prime example. More typically, the first person narrator tells us the story and does provide some context (is aware that he or she is telling a story), but is limited in what he or she can reveal by what he or she knows at the moment.

More commonly, first person narration is told in past tense, yet even here there are degrees of distance. We might call a first person narrator *reflective* if the story is told in the past tense. The narrator tells the story after the events of the story have taken place. This may be a few hours later or several days or weeks. However long it has been, the narrator now has had some time for reflection. She can put the story in context and decide for herself which events were the most important. She may even have some knowledge of events that she didn't witness, and she can reveal that knowledge to the reader. It is likely that a reflective narrator will have more commentary on the story, whereas an immediate narrator has less time to interpret the story, since it is still ongoing.

I like to call an extreme form of reflective narration *removed* first person narration. The further away from the events of the story the narrator is in time, the more information he or she can know about them. A removed narrator may have heard the story from several different characters' perspectives. He or she may know almost as much as an omniscient narrator, and may be able to give multiple perspectives on the story. He or she knows more than just the end of the story, but also knows how that "ending" affected the lives of the characters much, much later. And yet, the further removed the narrator is in time, the more memory can play tricks on him or her. He may become less reliable or there may be gaps in the story that she can no longer recollect. The struggle for memory or the search for the truth in memory may become as great a theme as the events of the story themselves.

Similarly, in third person, the author has several options to choose among. Traditionally, the most common has been third person *omniscient*, where the narrator knows everything that happened to all of the characters at all times. An omniscient narrator can be handy because there is nothing you can't tell, yet it can also be problematic because the reader may feel cheated if you don't reveal important information. With an omniscient narrator there are variations in *depth* as well. The omniscient narrator may reveal only external images about the story: description, action, and dialogue. This type of narration is often referred to as *cinematic*, since it is like a camera following the actions of the characters. On the other hand, the omniscient narrator can also reveal the thoughts of the characters, sometimes limiting this to the immediate surface thoughts or at other times delving into the innermost thoughts, fears, dreams, and emotions of the character.

More recent fiction has tended toward third person *limited* narration. Here, the narrator follows one focal character and tells only what that character thinks and experiences. The narrator may reveal only external images and dialogue or may reveal the character's thought in more or less depth. The only way the reader can find out about the thoughts and experiences of the other characters is through dialogue. Third person limited narration functions almost like first person, except that it is a little more distant, since we do not know who the narrator is as a character.

Like a first person narrator, in both omniscient and limited third person, the narrator can choose whether or not to comment on the story or the characters.

Since the narrator is usually not a character in a drama (with notable exceptions, of course), drama usually functions like cinematic third person narration. In other words, we see the events of the story unfold, but learn about the thoughts of the characters only through their dialogue. A playwright may choose to limit the scenes in a play to those in which one character plays a role, making the play more like limited third person, or she may choose to present scenes with all of the characters, where no one character is on stage all of the time, presenting a more or less omniscient perspective.

Similarly, in a poem we often expect a first person speaker, a personal reflection on an image or a situation. Yet many poets have rebelled against the autobiographical or confessional poem and have written poems in third or even second person. The voice in a poem may take a broad, even geological perspective and be relatively omniscient, encompassing thousands of years of history, perhaps. Or the voice may be limited to the observations of the speaker in the "present time" of the poem. In other words, though scholars of literature have developed a more extensive vocabulary for point of view in fiction than in other forms of writing, the same issues affect a poem, play, movie, essay, or personal narrative, though the limitations of the form may affect the writer's options for point of view as well.

Finally, for centuries writers have experimented with alternating perspectives within a text. An early example would be the *epistolary novel*, a first person narrative woven out of the letters of two (or more) characters to one another. The letters are each written in the first person, but they alternate between characters. Of course, in this form, the narrator is also limited, not only in terms of how much information he or she has access to, but also in terms of how much he or she is willing to reveal to the recipient of the letter. Alternating journal entries, or in a more contemporary setting blog entries or tweets, might be other ways to weave two or more first person perspectives together. In any case, the reader is not the intended audience for the fictional message, and that fact may have an effect on what is said and how it is said, since the message is addressed to another character.

It is also possible to alternate perspectives in third person narration without going so far as full omniscience, as long as the point where the perspective shifts is clearly delineated. Often in a novel with alternating perspectives, one chapter is told from one character's perspective and the next chapter is told from a different character's perspective. In a short story, clearly defined sections may be told in limited third person from different characters' points of view. Though this can be disorienting at first, most readers will catch on, if the transitions are handled well enough. It does take some practice, though, and probably isn't advisable in your first short story.

Problems with point of view arise when a first person narrator or a limited third person narrator reveals information that he or she cannot know. Often this will be the thought or feeling of another character. The writer knows what all the characters are thinking, but forgets for a moment that the narrator he or she has chosen does not know as much as the writer does.

This happens a lot in the early drafts of stories and even poems, and it may be marked "POV" in a draft. What is meant by this is that the point of view shifts at this point in the story—sometimes an early draft will even switch between first and third person narration. It doesn't mean that the story is flawed, only that the issue of point of view is working itself out, and you have some choices to make.

Do you switch back and forth between first and third or even second person? Maybe you are searching for the right voice for the narrator. Once you decide which comes more naturally for you in this story, then you can go back and revise the other sections. Did your narrator reveal information that she cannot know? Maybe you need to consider whether to use an omniscient narrator or, if the narration is told in the first person, consider when the story is told. Would there be any way for your narrator to have access to that information by the point she tells the story? How omniscient do you want the narrator to be? How much information should you reveal and how much can you withhold before your narrator loses credibility with the reader? Do you want a reliable narrator or are you interested in a narrator that does withhold information (and how can you as author tip the narrator's hand to the reader by including evidence that calls his version of events into question). In early drafts, writers tend to experiment with point of view subconsciously. There's nothing wrong with that. Maybe you're used to one form of storytelling, but your subconscious mind is telling you to experiment with another. The only major problem with point of view is inconsistency, but that is only a real problem in the final draft.

✦ Writing Journal Exercises

1. Return to the public place you described in a previous assignment. This time, try to describe it from the perspective of someone else who is present. Consider the aspects of the place that they have access to and what they would experience. Consider their needs and interests and how these would affect the way they perceive the space. You may try to write in this person's voice, or you may choose an impersonal third person narrator who portrays the experience through the lens of this person as a character.

2. Retell your family story in third person with an omniscient narrator or a limited narrator focused on someone other than yourself. You may choose to write external, cinematic narration or internal narration that reveals one or more characters' thoughts and emotions.

3. Retell a folk tale, myth, or legend from a new perspective. Take on the "villain's" or "loser's" point of view or write from the perspective of an insignificant character (maybe even an invented character who could have been present but isn't mentioned in the original). Or rewrite a male-oriented story from a female or other perspective. What details might the new point-of-view character notice? What new insights can this new perspective reveal?

4. Take a passage you have written in either first person or third person and rewrite it using the other form of narration. If you used "I," then write about the experience, but describe the "I" from a distance, using he or she. If you have written the passage in third person, then take on one of the characters as the narrator and write from his or her perspective, using the pronoun "I" to refer to the narrator. Write in that character's voice.

5. Write a passage two ways: The first time write it in present tense as if it is happening at the moment (or as if you are reliving it in the moment through memory). The second time, write the passage in the past tense, as if you are recollecting what happened. In the first passage, try to write with little reflection, only allowing the kind of reflection you might have in the moment and limiting your knowledge to what you know at the time. In the second passage, allow yourself the opportunity to comment on the action as you would if you were telling about it some time later and had time to think about it.

6. Choose an emotion. Write a passage that portrays that emotion without naming and without allowing a character in the passage to name it in dialogue. In fact, dialogue should be fairly limited in the passage, though a character may say a few words in response to another. Try to evoke the emotion through description of the setting, description of the character(s), the actions and expressions of the character(s), and the light or other actions in the surroundings. In other words, write the passage using a cinematic narrator who only reveals what the camera can see and hear, though you may also describe scent, touch, and even taste.

7. Write a page or more in the voice of one character describing another character. For the character whose voice you take on, choose someone who is not the main character. The character described can be a main character or any other character. Write about something the character did and the way that the character acts. The character describing the other character can refer to him or herself as "I" in the passage. The character describing may refer to the other character as "you" or as "he" or "she."

8. Describe a place first from a panoramic viewpoint. Imagine you are looking at it from far away. Then zoom in on one part of the scene and describe it in detail. Again, focus in on a different part of the scene. You might make a smooth or abrupt transition between close-ups. Try a mid-range or macro camera angle for another part of the scene.

9

Finding Patterns

Beginnings of Form

At some point in the writing process, the writer will move beyond the initial stages of generating ideas and begin to shape those ideas into a story, poem, play, or essay. Though we are moving toward those bigger forms and to our discussion of specific genre conventions, it seems worthwhile to stop for a moment and consider how a writer makes that choice and how to begin to give those ideas some structure. In a way, the previous two chapters have already invited you to do this. By exploring character and by making choices in perspective or point of view, you may already have brought some definition to a story or poem. You have begun to move beyond ideas *for* a work that you might write, and you have begun to think of it *as* a work in progress.

It's likely you already know whether the work is shaping up as a poem, story, play, or essay.

However, if you're not sure which genre to choose, consider whether the characters and their actions are most important to what you are writing. If so, then it's likely you have started on a story. If, on the other hand, the sound of the words and the emotions and ideas evoked by the images are most central, then you have likely begun a poem. The choice of whether to tell a story as fiction, nonfiction, or drama may be made due to the form you are most familiar with or interested in. The choice of essay or poem may depend in part on the voice you adopt. In truth, nearly any idea can be developed in any form: there are narrative poems, even long epics or plays and novels in verse, there is flash fiction or prose poetry, there are epigrams or aphorisms that bridge the gap between non-fiction and poetry, and there is just about everything in between.

So in this chapter, I will invite you to rethink your initial choices, even of genre, and explore formal patterns on their own before making a final choice of genre.

Development and Revision

This is a good time to talk some more about development and revision. As we said in Chapter 2, you often start writing by just trying to get some ideas on paper, but you don't worry much about form, about point of view, etc. Once you have all or part of a piece written down, you have to start making decisions about where you're headed. Some people write all the way to an endpoint, then go back and reshape, writing what is called a *zero draft* that doesn't have to be perfect but does explore the essential shape. They write quickly, knowing that they can go back later and fill in the details. Other people write a little bit, then reshape, to get a sense of where the end might lie. It may take these writers several incomplete attempts before they find the pattern they want to reach a conclusion. There's no one right answer for everyone.

Whether you are somewhere in the middle of an idea or whether you've completed one draft of it, one way to get a sense of its structure is to write an *outline*. That sounds like the kind of analytical thinking you might use in expository writing, but it doesn't have to be. Instead, think of an outline as any kind of sketch of your ideas. William Faulkner wrote on the walls of his office in Rowan Oak to outline his novels. One is still there, and you can see it if you go and visit his home. You might think of an outline as a timeline or a chronology that shows all of the events of a story as they unfold in real (fictional) time. Or you might outline the order of scenes as you want them to appear in the story. As we shall see, these do not have to be identical. Both kinds of outline can be helpful if you decide not to tell the story in chronological order. Having a chronological map of the story will help you keep the story straight when you rearrange the way you tell it.

The shape of your outline doesn't matter, either. You might write something more akin to an idea map or a sketch. Movie scripts are often drawn out on storyboards with stick figures or cartoon characters to represent the scene. You might use butcher paper to write on, or outlining or project planning software, or you might write lists in your journal: list the scenes in a story and include what changes in each scene or why the scene needs to be shown.

Another option, besides an outline, is a *collage* approach. In this strategy, you take what you have written, cut it up, and piece the resulting fragments together, trying out different orders until you find the one you like best. Some writers actually use scissors to cut up what they've written and rearrange it, line by line or paragraph by paragraph. Others use a word processor to do the same thing (remember to save a copy of the file before you mess with it too much). Putting the pieces of what you've written together in a new order can help you see new connections between them, even if you go back to the original order eventually. Some writers don't try to write a complete draft initially. They write in sections until they think they have enough to work with, then try to find different combinations and orders until they find the one they like.

Whether you write a complete draft and then re-examine its structure, or whether you write in pieces and then put it together, it is likely that you will find passages that don't really fit the new structure once you're aware of it. You may have needed to write a scene for a story or a stanza of a poem to get you to the next step, but if it's not adding enough to the story or poem, you need to have the courage to cut it out. If you really like it, but it isn't working where it is, keep a copy. You might use it in a different place later or it might become the genesis of something new.

As you examine the structure of your piece, you will likely find passages that didn't get written (such as a scene you need or a transition that got skipped over), which you'll need to develop further. To do this may mean going back to the drawing board and re-imagining those parts. You may need to do research or go back to the source of your inspiration to find out what you need to add. Making those additions may change the balance of the piece and cause you to cut something somewhere else or to shift parts around some more.

Writing takes a lot of courage—revision takes even more. You've got to be willing to cut out over half of the draft you just wrote, to take that character you love from scene 3 and save him or her for another story, to take the image in stanza 2 and write a different poem with it, and to take all the dead, boring language that got you to the story, image, etc. and cut it out. You've also got to be willing to add the things that got left out the first time around and not just accept it for what it is because it is written. Revision means having the guts to re-envision what you've written and change it drastically, even if that may not be absolutely necessary, but might make it better.

How do you know where to cut and where to add? Obviously, one thing to look at is the language and imagery. Where that's working, keep it. But be honest: when it's not good enough, cut it. Another way is to go back and look at the shape of what you've written. What basic shape is the work taking on? Would another shape be better?

One element of form is balance. If you have a long stanza at the beginning of the poem, do you need an equally long stanza toward the end for balance? Or does your poem get gradually smaller as it reaches the end (and is there a reason why it should)? If you have a short introductory scene, do you need a short closing scene, instead of a long one? Or do you need to go back and add some to the first scene?

Of course, as with all the "rules" of form, this is made to be broken. There are many ways of looking at balance besides exact, equal symmetry. Those of you who have studied classical painting might remember the ratios used: the harmonic ratio of 6:8:12 is reflected in the sonnet's octet and sestet. Asymmetry can be just as effective as symmetry, though the effects will differ. Often an odd number feels like a satisfying series: plays commonly are written with one act, three acts, or five, but I can't remember the last two act or six act play I've seen (which is not to say that it can't be done).

Often we start writing where we need to in order to understand the material, but the reader could start later and then fill in just enough of that information. How much of your first scene could be woven into the piece as backstory? Would the action pick up sooner if you cut a scene or two at the beginning? Or did you write past the ending? Might the reader be satisfied or more engaged if all of the loose ends aren't tied up? But maybe you have given up before the end, and the story needs another scene or two, or you found an easy place to end the poem, but the tensions you started with haven't been fully resolved. Does your ending make the reader re-evaluate the story or poem and want to re-read it with the ending in mind?

Story Forms

Whether you write in prose or in poetry or drama, a story is likely to follow a pattern; it is not a random series of events, even if we find it in what appears to be or may actually be random events. If I told you everything that happened to me over the course of a day, it probably wouldn't sound very interesting, but if I tell you the story of my day, then I select what I'm going to tell you and what moments of my day are important to the story. I emphasize certain moments and leave out others that seem trivial. The actions of one moment seem like the causes of the things that occur in the next moment (even if some unrelated things actually happened in between). Those actions lead me to the conclusion of the story, even if, in reality, life generally keeps on going. A story, then, is a selection of events related as a narrative that reaches some kind of conclusion. I could probably tell a different story about the same day by selecting different events or relating them in a different way, and the meaning I might derive from the story would change in the telling.

The most basic model of a story (or any form, really) is that it must have a beginning, a middle, and an end. We start the story somewhere, but how to know where to start? We tell about some things in the middle, but how do we choose what to tell? We stop telling the story at some point, but how do we know when we've reached the end? Established forms can help us make these decisions—or if we strike out on our own, we can at least learn from the established forms that have come before.

Stories are about change. If nothing changes, then we say nothing happens, and we haven't reached a conclusion. So often, stories start where the change starts. Something disrupts the status quo, the characters respond to that disruption throughout the middle of the story where there may also be complications (other changes that result from the initial one), until in the conclusion a new status quo (however tentative or unsatisfying) is reached. Something, however minimal, has changed. It may not last. It may not resolve every conflict. But something changes in a story. It may be that the characters change the world around them. It may be that the characters are changed by the events of the story. One way to illustrate this is with the *narrative arc.*

Narrative Arc

Crisis

(Falling Action)
Resolution

Rising Action
Complications
Tensions Build

Exposition

Since Aristotle wrote his *Poetics* describing the art of poetry and drama, some version of this basic model has often been used to describe how stories work. In the beginning, there is some exposition that establishes the lay of the land and the central conflict. In the middle of the story there is rising action as tensions build and complications are introduced, which lead to a crisis. Often the crisis is followed by some falling action, as tensions decrease, though this is usually shorter than the rising action and it may not be necessary at all. The end comes with some form of resolution, though it need not be a full resolution.

If tensions do not build to a crisis, which provides a focus for the story, then no resolution is possible. The crisis may be dramatic or subtle, the rising action may be gradual or steep, the resolution may be for the better or for the worse, but some movement, some change must occur in a story. Yet how to reach that point of change can be a challenge as you start a story. One strategy is to model the story around a familiar pattern.

One such pattern is a *journey*. What happens on a journey? You leave one place and arrive at another. Along the way, many episodes can occur. There may be obstacles to overcome or there may be detours, but the destination is always in sight. There is no guarantee of reaching the destination, of course, but it does give the journey a purpose and direction, and when you do reach it, probably after some crisis, you know you've reached the resolution. Or if the crisis diverts you from the destination, you may end up somewhere unexpected.

An actual journey takes place in time and space, yet we also think in terms of a psychological journey, so this model could be useful whether or not the characters in your story travel any distance. In a psychological journey, you begin in one state of mind, encounter several obstacles, episodes, and detours along the way, and end up in a new mental state.

A variation on the typical journey might be the *quest*. Instead of knowing where you are going on a quest, you only know what you are looking for, though that could be as ambiguous as "adventure." As with a journey, you likely encounter several obstacles, detours, distractions, or other episodes before (possibly) finding the object of the quest and returning home. Maybe the biggest difference between a journey and a quest is that the journey takes you away and the quest brings you home, but you have been changed in the process.

Yet another pattern for a story might be called a *visitation*. This is when a new character arrives on the scene and disrupts the status quo. Think of the archetypal Western. A new sheriff arrives in town or a tall, dark, and handsome cowboy rides in. The sheriff has to enforce the law and clean up all the outlaws in the town, saving one or two townsfolk along the way. Or the cowboy comes to town and takes on the corrupt sheriff and his gang. There is plenty of conflict, but once all the bad guys have been rounded up and the town is safe again, the cowboy rides off into the sunset or the sheriff is assigned to another town.

Certainly, these aren't the only patterns for stories, though they are common ones that have been successfully adapted many times. To find others, all you have to do is read. Folk tales can be a valuable source. Consider the pattern of the worthy young woman who loses her status (her father remarries after her mother dies), she has to endure suffering and often is banished, but then with the aid of magic or her own resourcefulness, she is able to regain her status, usually first by taking on a disguise, but eventually, her true identity is revealed.

Rhetorical and Poetic Forms

Story isn't the only model you might use in your writing, of course. Many kinds of creative writing take their cue from rhetoric or logical argument to find a structure. The rhetorical pattern of thesis, antithesis, and conclusion can be mirrored in an essay, story, poem, or play. An essay may make an explicit argument, but a story or poem may be a bit more subtle about it. Rather than presenting a thesis, you might think in terms of point, counterpoint, and resolution. You might write with one type of imagery or present one type of character initially, then contrast that with its opposite (or at least something strikingly different), and finally find a way to resolve the two differences at least partly.

Poetic forms like the sonnet, with its rhetorical turn or *volta* in the ninth line, rely on this kind of logic. The antagonist and protagonist create a kind of argument that may be acted out by the characters of a story or play. Logic can be used for structure, even if the content you are writing about is inherently illogical or emotional.

Some forms in poetry use intricate rhyme schemes or repetition to weave these contrasts together. The villanelle repeats the first and third line as the last line of alternating stanzas until both come back again in the final stanza. The sestina repeats the same six final words in each stanza in an intricate pattern that uses them in every possible combination. By the end, it is nearly impossible to predict how those words will be used, yet with each repetition, the words are used with a different shade of meaning. Form affects or limits the content, in other words. Certain poetic forms have traditional subjects, which a modern poet may follow or write against. For instance, the sonnet was traditionally a poem about love or religious devotion (or both), though a modern poet might write an anti-love sonnet.

Finding a pre-existing pattern can also help you develop the middle of your story or poem. It can suggest the kinds of complications and even the crisis that your character might encounter. You may find that following a form in poetry takes you to subjects you wouldn't have conceived of on your own. If you haven't completed the pattern, then you have to keep writing until you do.

Or you may find that form limits what you can say in productive ways. Sometimes less is more, and to face the challenge of fitting your ideas within the confines of a form can mean you have to distill the absolutely essential words and ideas.

That doesn't mean that you have to adhere slavishly to the pattern. Literature lives off variation and adaptation. You might decide to rewrite a fairy tale or to sidetrack the character on a quest, so she never makes it home, but does find what she's looking for. Or you may decide to invent your own forms by writing in free verse, but some pattern will emerge in your writing, and that pattern may need to be reinforced or refined as you polish your draft. Knowing the patterns of existing forms can help you decide what works and what doesn't when you strike out on your own to invent a form. In the end, you may rely on your intuition to determine the right form, but your intuition is informed by your knowledge and your understanding of the tradition you are writing in or against.

✒ Writing Journal Exercises

1. Take a poem you've written and try a collage technique. Write the poem out on a separate piece of paper, then cut the poem up into pieces (literally). Each piece should have a line, a phrase, or an image on it. Then rearrange the pieces on a surface, looking for a new order and for interesting connections. Be willing to change line lengths. Try combining two lines into one or cutting a line in two if it is long. Your lines do not have to be even or arranged flush left on the page. Look for an interesting visual arrangement. Then tape or paste the pieces into your journal in this order (or if you'd rather, you can copy the poem out in this pattern).

2. Write an outline of a story or poem you either have written or are planning to write. In your outline, for a story, list the main scenes and briefly note what happens in each scene or, for a poem, summarize the topic of each stanza by listing the central image or idea. Is the outline balanced? Is it too symmetrical? Consider adding one or more

stanzas or scenes. Where might it go? Consider cutting out one or more stanzas or scenes. Which might be superfluous? You may find you need to delete some and add some.

3. Write an outline of a journey you've been on. What was your starting point and what was your destination? What steps did you take along the way? If you were to write this as a story, what obstacles, detours, or complications might you add to give the story more tension? Add these to your outline. How would they affect the way you reach the destination (or whether you do reach it) and how might those obstacles affect the characters and their outcome.

4. Consider that one of your characters is on a quest. What are they literally trying to find? What abstract quality might this thing represent (to them or to the reader)? What lengths is your character willing to go in order to complete the quest? What obstacles might stand in the character's way and what might these obstacles represent? What challenges are placed in the character's path that make it possible for her or him to gain the qualities needed to achieve the final goal? How has your character changed when (or if) s/he returns?

5. Consider a setting you might write about. Describe the static conditions in that setting as they might exist at the outset of a story or poem. Who might arrive on the scene, and how might their appearance disrupt the status quo? What forces in the setting would be antagonistic to the newcomer? What characters might be allies or might need to be "rescued" by the newcomer? What would the locals learn about their situation due to the arrival of the visitor? What would mark the end of the visitation?

6. Take an idea from your journal that you started as a story. Write it as a poem. It might still be a narrative poem with a hint of story to it, or it might be more descriptive of a character or a place. Don't worry yet about the form of the poem. Just write it in lines and try to distill the original idea down to its essence. Maybe you're trying to get at a character trait. Maybe you're trying to capture an emotion without telling the full story. You might go back later and develop the story as fiction, but for now, try to capture one element of it. Pay attention to the sounds and rhythms of the language and look for interesting word combinations.

7. Take an idea from your journal that you started as a poem. Consider who is the speaker of that poem and what the situation might be in which the poem is said. If it were part of a dialogue, who might be listening? Why would the speaker say the poem? Rewrite as either an outline of the story that would lead up to or result from the speaking of the poem, or as a passage of dramatic dialogue between the characters who might hear the poem. Of course, the language of the poem might change as you rewrite it in prose or the poem itself might never be uttered.

8. Take an exercise that you began as nonfiction. Consider how you might develop it as fiction or drama. Add characters to the setting or, if there are characters in the exercise, allow them to be different from their real-life counterparts. Sketch out what might happen to these characters if they were to interact with another fully fictional character who might provide interesting contrasts or tensions.

10

Creative Nonfiction

What Is Creative Nonfiction?

On the one hand, the answer to this question is easy: The term "nonfiction" suggests that it is the opposite of fiction. But then where do poetry and drama fit in? They are also not fiction (and some libraries classify them under nonfiction), yet we see them as distinct from nonfiction.

Nonfiction may mean that it is true, factual, not "made up," though as we'll see, even that can be problematic. But in general, the goal of nonfiction is to stick to reality rather than invent it.

So what makes some nonfiction creative? We might say that creative nonfiction is literary nonfiction, but what does that mean? One answer is that it's not only about what it says it's about. I might write about my childhood to reveal something about race relations or I might write a travelogue of Paris, not to be a guidebook to the city, but to present a guide to French culture or compare it to my culture. Or I might write a recipe, not to cook it (though maybe you could) but to get at the philosophy or way of life of my grandmother.

In other words, one difference between creative nonfiction and other kinds of nonfiction revolves around purpose. The purpose of an essay is generally to inform or to persuade. Creative nonfiction can do both of those things, but it also looks deeper. Let's say I want to write a manual on how to use hand tools: that's nonfiction. But if my purpose is to ponder a lost way of life, then it's creative nonfiction. As you might guess, purpose can be a gray area. How do we know what the author intended? A lot may depend on what the reader can get out of the work, based on the tone and the voice as much as the content.

Another distinction between creative nonfiction and regular nonfiction is based not on why it is written, but on how it is written. We might say that creative nonfiction is more concerned with how it is written than what it is about. Though of course content matters, form is a bigger issue in creative nonfiction than in other types of nonfiction. In creative nonfiction, like in other literary genres, a word is chosen, not only for what it means, but also based on its sound or connotations.

We might combine both of these distinctions by saying that creative nonfiction uses literary techniques to add multiple layers of content to nonfiction. This is not to say that creative nonfiction is necessarily better than other forms of nonfiction, just that it is different. I might enjoy reading a literary phone book more than I would a regular phonebook, but if I wanted to look up a number, I'd still turn to the White Pages. A personal essay on the effects of global warming might really bring the issues home and make me care about them, but if I really want to understand the science behind the theories, I might want to look at articles in scientific journals.

Perhaps the most essential forms of creative nonfiction are the essay and the story, judging from the two most common types, the personal essay and the memoir. Both of these forms often stem from personal experience and are based in fact. For example, memoir is a dialogue with the author's past, and thus relies more heavily on story. Personal essay is a dialogue with the reader, and may use more argument or analysis. But both forms can use elements of the other. A personal essay may tell a story as evidence to back up a point the writer wants to make. A memoir may start out with a story, but then include some logical argument like you would find in an essay. Both forms rely heavily on image and voice, which also ties them to poetry, and like poetry, creative nonfiction often juxtaposes images, puts them side by side with little or no commentary, and allows the reader to decide.

Like fiction, creative nonfiction develops scenes through concrete description that develops in the moment. It also can make use of characters who come alive more than in a news report, for instance. Yet in creative nonfiction, we also are more likely to allow the author to tell what she or he is thinking than we would in either fiction or poetry. As in an essay that contains a thesis, even in memoir, we read to find the author's take on the situation. Since the emphasis is more on what the author has to say, the focus may be less on plot and more on thought. You don't have to rely on rising tension, conflict, crisis, and resolution because you get that in the argument of the essay or the realizations found in memoir.

Memoir

In memoir the writer goes back to an episode from his or her past. While autobiography is a relatively complete account of the writer's life, memoir generally limits itself to a specific time and place. A memoir may be shorter than an autobiography or it may simply set more limits on the amount of time covered in order to explore that time more thoroughly. Memoir also often explores the role memory plays in our understanding of the past, and the writer's present understanding is often as important to the memoir as the past events themselves. Telling the story of the past is important, of course, but the way that story is revealed in memoir is often shaped by the struggle to remember and to come to terms with those past events, so a straightforward chronological story is not always the best or only choice.

   The memoir may begin with a strong memory, setting the scene and evoking the mood of that past, or it may begin in the present and work its way back in memory. The past events may seem murky and elusive or the clarity of memory may be what compels the narrative. The differences between past and present may be the main subject of the story, or the subject may be the attempt to explore the workings of memory and come to terms with your past.

   To write memoir, you may need nothing more than your own memories, of course, though many writers find old photographs or objects from that time and place evoke the memories and fill in some of the details. Visiting a place from your past may also call up memories and help you navigate the passage from present to past. Talking to others who were involved in the events or who know the place you are writing about can also help bring back memories and broaden your perspective. Including detailed descriptions of the relics from that time and place and including interviews or conversations in your narrative may help bring that time to life. And the writer often takes a step forward and reflects on the act of memoir or comments on the lessons learned in remembering.

Literary Biography and Family History

Of course, writers do not have to limit themselves only to their own experience. The literary biography is a form that attempts to dramatize the events of someone's life, to tell their story as if it were fiction, while remaining as true as possible to the facts. It differs from the biographical novel in that less license is taken with characters and events, yet the moments of a life are told in scenic detail with dialogue that may be true to life, but usually must be invented.

Though it is possible to research a historical figure in enough detail to write a literary biography, that is often a much bigger task than can be accomplished in a few weeks, unless you take a very brief episode in the figure's life to write about. Instead, it may be more manageable to write the story of a family member, friend, or someone in your town. Start by interviewing the person to collect their oral history. Bring a video camera or audio recorder so you can get a complete record. You may want to focus your interview around a particular time or event or a role the person played in the community. Talk to others who knew the person to get their perspective. If you can't conduct interviews in person, correspond by email or letters or go back through old family histories, letters, or photographs to piece together the parts of the story you don't know.

When writing biography or history as creative nonfiction, include as many details as you can from your research, but weave them together to create a scene that allows the characters to speak in dialogue or describe their actions as if they were characters in fiction. As in memoir, you can also step forward as the narrator and comment or reflect on the person and the events. The story may be organized as much around your reflections as around the chronology of events, and the conclusion may not come from crisis and resolution as in a story, but from the coming together of those reflections in a deeper understanding of your subject.

Travel Narrative

Not all stories told in creative nonfiction deal with the past. Many stories deal with the present, and a common subject for creative nonfiction is the travel narrative. Here, rather than traveling in memory, the writer literally travels to another place to explore what differences in culture or setting can reveal about that place and about herself. As with the personal essay or memoir, the travel narrative is not only a description of the place, but is also self-reflective. The impact the place has on the writer or the impact that travel has is important. Whereas in a travel guide the most important point would be to accurately portray a city or country, while giving advice on the sights to see and places to eat or stay, in the travel narrative the experience of the traveler is tantamount, and the details of the place illustrate that experience.

Often the travel narrative might be written in the form of a journal as if it were recorded in real time during the journey, and this may be a good strategy for writing one. A certain level of editing and shaping will obviously be done after the fact, to comment on the experience or at least edit out the less interesting moments and focus on the details that give the narrative a structure and some semblance of plot.

Other travel narratives read more like memoir, though the time between the travel and the writing may be less. A reflective story or essay about a trip you've taken in the past year or two will still sound more immediate than memoir, and yet you will have had more time for reflection than if you wrote a journal during your trip. Consider why you went there, and compare the place you went to the place you live now or the rhythms of your life on the road to the rhythms of your daily life now. Compare the place you expected to find with the one you actually experienced.

What discoveries about the place or about yourself did you make while traveling, and how has your sense of self or place changed since returning home? The travel narrative may read more like a story or more like a personal essay with story elements.

Personal Essay

The personal essay, like any essay, may include a thesis and main points to support the thesis, but the organization of the essay is likely to be less structured. It will often present an inductive argument, rather than a deductive one. It may tell a story as an example of the point the writer is trying to make, then give some factual evidence to add context to the story, and draw a conclusion based on the evidence. Personal essay often relies on anecdote to add the personal to the factual. It may begin with a question or just with an observation, rather than a distinct thesis, and its conclusion may not be as definite as the conclusion of an expository essay. Its strength is that it explores the human side of the equation. It looks at an issue and makes that issue come alive for the reader.

When writing a personal essay, you may well make use of common expository essay strategies, such as comparison and contrast, making a definition, analyzing cause and effect, or making a persuasive argument. Still, the emphasis in creative nonfiction tends to be more focused on the experience of the writer than on the argument with the reader. The story of how the writer arrived at her conclusions may be as important and persuasive as the facts of the argument themselves. We are interested in the personal journey of the writer, as much as we are in the subject of the essay, though that is still of interest. The conclusion of a personal essay may be less definite than in an expository essay, yet the willingness of the writer to consider a subject from many angles without insisting on one right way to view it can also lend the writer credence.

To write a personal essay, choose a subject you already have a strong connection with or find an unfamiliar subject that you are willing to immerse yourself in. You might start with the experience that led you to this subject and describe your fascination. Conduct research, both by using library and internet searches to read about your subject and by finding ways to gain hands-on experience. Weave together the facts and the experience, and fill your essay with concrete scenic detail, yet also allow yourself room to express your thought or make an argument.

True Crime and New Journalism

Like literary biography, family history or the personal essay, true crime and new journalism use the techniques of fiction to dramatize a story from the news, whether that is to document the details of a crime or to report on another event or cultural phenomenon. Story technique is used to bring the facts to life and transport the reader to that time and place. As in a travel narrative, the role of the writer is often examined, and the impact of the story is felt first on the writer and then by the reader. In other words, the writer is not always an objective observer as we at least attempt to be in reporting the news, but the writer's subjective reflections are equally part of the story.

To truly explore a crime or other news story takes the skills and the time of the reporter. True crime writers may spend months with court documents and eye-witness reports, and they may also hit the streets to interview subjects, victims, and family members, often putting themselves in dangerous situations. Though it may be too much of a challenge right now to investigate a murder or other violent crime, you might consider investigating a local news story that is a little more accessible and less dangerous, and writing the story behind the story by bringing it to life. Or you might consider investigating a cultural phenomenon like a local festival, a concert, a beauty pageant, or a protest rally and combining news-style reporting with scenic portrayal and lyric descriptions of the people and places you witness.

This kind of writing might lead to social commentary or even satire, when objective reporting becomes less prominent than personal or philosophical reflection. Social commentary describes and analyzes events, movements, groups, and communities. Satire takes the analysis one step further and critiques its subject, often by using hyperbole and humor. Though satire might introduce fictional elements, it is always with an eye toward an actual situation that the satirist aims to change. This kind of writing has a history going back at least as far as Joseph Addison's and Richard Steele's essays in *The Spectator* or Jonathan Swift's "A Modest Proposal."

Lyric Essay

When we think of an essay, we tend to think of a piece of prose with a thesis, a conclusion, and at least some form of argument. The essay usually has a point it is trying to reach, and it may get to that point with a logical, deductive argument or by induction, finding its way to a conclusion through intuition more than through logic. And yet there is a fairly straightforward rhetorical path with a definite conclusion.

This is not the case with the lyric essay, a term that may seem like an oxymoron. The lyric essay uses prose in combination with the strategies of poetry as a form of meditation on its object. It does not create a narrative, nor does it attempt an argument. The lyric essay often presents us with a collage of short, fragmentary passages that each explore an image, a set of facts, an anecdote, etc. As in a poem, the play with language and image is important, and the reader is left to form his or her own conclusions about the subject.

The lyric essay is evocative, but not overtly persuasive; it explores its subject deeply, yet does no more than suggest a conclusion. The material of the essay is not presented as evidence to prove a point, in other words, but is simply presented, pondered, and juxtaposed alongside other kinds of information. The writer may intrude less than in the personal essay, though passages of anecdote or memoir are often mixed with more objective or scientific observations, lists of data, or news accounts.

One strategy for organizing this type of essay is the *braid*. In this type of writing, which might also be used for a memoir, personal essay, poetry, or fiction, three or more strands of content are intertwined throughout the piece. A lyric essay may take a series of anecdotes about the subject from the author's life, and alternate telling those bits of memoir with a series of reflections on the history of the subject, then weave in a series of passages that list or describe the objective facts of the subject, perhaps statistical data or scientific observations. Each strand of the essay may have its own distinctive style and voice, yet they are all unified around the central subject. Each strand reflects on the other by association and without direct commentary. Though the same essay might be written in three discrete sections that each explore one aspect of the subject, weaving the strands together highlights the connections and allows readers to discover them on their own.

Flash Nonfiction

If you take the lyric essay or memoir and distill it to its most essential qualities, you will have flash nonfiction, a very brief essay or memoir. Guidelines for length vary anywhere from under 250 words to under 1,000 words. With such restrictions there is little room to do anything more than suggest an argument, so typically the flash piece is short on rhetoric and long on revelation. The flash writer dwells in concrete and specific detail, and the essay or story must grab the reader's attention in the very first sentence and sustain that level of intensity through the closing word. There is precious little time for explanation or contemplation, as the writer lays down one perception after another, suggesting an interpretation but rarely verbalizing it. As in the poem or in flash fiction, the goal is to say as much with as few words as possible and to rely as much on what isn't said as what is.

Yet length is not the only thing that distinguishes flash nonfiction. It is also distinguished by intensity. The flash essay isn't usually a fragment of a longer piece; instead, it attempts to accomplish everything that a memoir or essay does on a smaller canvas. The scene and the tensions of the piece must be established immediately, and those tensions play out quickly and dramatically. As in poetry, there is often more emphasis on the sound and texture of the language. Sentence structure and the flow of sentences across a paragraph are also important when every word counts. As in flash fiction, the essential structure of a story and the suggestion of a character from the smallest details can give the essay life. Like the lyric essay, flash nonfiction can make use of the white space between paragraphs to suggest what hasn't been revealed and leap from one experience to the next with few or no transitions. Though this may lead to a conclusion that is open-ended and fragmentary, there is, nonetheless, some sense of closure.

In this case, readers don't feel they've been given only part of the equation; instead, they are left pondering the fragmentary nature of some truths.

Truth in Nonfiction

Creative nonfiction shares many qualities with the other genres we are studying. In all forms of creative nonfiction, true life events are dramatized as they would be in fiction, yet the writer does not stray too far from what actually happened. Many poems arise from the same impulse as memoir or the personal essay. And even plays have been inspired by actual events and may involve the same kind of investigative reporting as new journalism to document the human side of an issue. In all of these cases, the main distinction between nonfiction and other forms may be the form, more than whether or not the details are "true."

We often think of nonfiction as being based in facts or being "true," whereas fiction is invented and therefore less true, even if it resembles the truth or may be emotionally "true" on a certain level. Once you start thinking about creative nonfiction, though, it becomes clear that it must take some liberties with the truth.

Consider memoir. How accurate and complete are your memories? No one has 100 percent total recall, so if you want to tell what happened on a given day, you will probably have to invent some of the details. The conversations that went on may have been like the ones you remember, but you probably don't remember them word for word. You might know (or research) what kinds of clothes people wore in that decade, but you likely don't know exactly what you wore that day.

You might leave some details out, of course, and focus on what you do remember, but even that distorts the truth by omission. On the other hand, if you claim that you did something important and in fact you never did, your readers might get angry if you call it nonfiction.

Besides the need to rely on invention to fill in the details and bring the known facts to life, the nonfiction writer makes use of many of the same conventions used by the fiction writer. In nonfiction, you might use telescoping to combine things that happened in several incidents into one scene. However, you may need to be careful not to distort the truth too much. If several inconsequential and repetitive actions occur in one scene of a memoir instead of over the course of several weeks in reality, that may not make much of a difference, but if two pivotal pieces of evidence are discovered at the same time in a true crime story, when in fact they were discovered weeks apart, that may affect the way we perceive the police as either inept or competent. In that case, telescoping those two events may seem like taking too much liberty.

Typically, readers will allow the nonfiction writer to take a few liberties with the facts, as long as the writer remains true to the experience. But sometimes taking liberties has gotten people in trouble. A well-known case was James Frey with *A Million Little Pieces*, a memoir that was revealed to be fiction and may have been initially marketed to publishers as a novel. Because the market for nonfiction was better and the story more believable as nonfiction, he changed what he labeled it, the theory goes. But when it was revealed that he had invented major parts of the story, that decision backfired. This goes to show that we expect a certain amount of truth in nonfiction, even though we know a writer has to imagine some of the details.

Of course, novelists draw on reality all the time, so if you are interested in writing about real events, the issue may be about what you should call it. Ravi Howard's book *Like Trees Walking* was researched and based on the 1980s lynching in Mobile, Alabama, yet he called it a novel because the characters are invented, even though the facts of the case are true. Truman Capote's *In Cold Blood* was marketed as a novel, though it is often seen as an early form of creative nonfiction, since it was based on interviews with the murderer of a farm family, as well as interviews with people in the town where the murders took place.

A lyric essay may dramatize certain moments, by including either memoir or biography, and we know that some of those moments may be imagined, not reported, yet the facts about the subject can't be invented, and any objective data that is woven into the essay needs to be objective and verifiable.

Writers often talk about the emotional truth of their writing. When memoirists work with memory to tell a story the way they remember it, rather than the way it happened, we get this kind of truth. Yet there must always be a good reason for bending the truth or inventing some details. Change too much, and you lose all credibility; change too little, and all the life may go out of the story. It is a fine tightrope to walk, and one writers will always argue about.

How to Revise Creative Nonfiction

Since creative nonfiction can take different forms, there is no one-size-fits-all approach. The personal essay may seem very different from the memoir, and the travelogue may face different issues from the lyric essay. Still, there are a number of issues you might consider for any kind of creative nonfiction.

Consider your use of concrete and specific images. Though there may be more room for abstract thought in a personal essay than in a poem or story, one of the things that makes the essay personal is the artist's vision, which often comes across best in the image. Similarly, in a memoir, the more vivid the imagery, the clearer and more interesting the memory is for the reader. Where you have abstract language, consider whether you could replace it or augment it with an image. This may be a single image that embodies the idea or an anecdote or scene that illustrates it.

Also consider the voice of the piece. Is it consistent throughout? Is it personal enough for your purpose? What would happen if you allowed more distance between your narrative voice and your subject? What would happen if you allowed yourself to be more personal or even more emotional about the subject? Do you make the transition between passages that use essay techniques and passages that tell a story?

If you are writing a personal essay, where might you use elements of memoir by telling part of a story? If your main focus is memoir, how might the observations allowed in the personal essay help you make a point or frame the narrative? Remember that a memoir often has a more intrusive narrator who comments or reflects. The conclusion of a memoir may come, not from crisis and resolution, but from reflection and summing up.

Consider the structure of your essay. Do you tell a straightforward, chronological narrative or does your narrator move back and forth in time? If you are writing memoir or a personal narrative, where might you weave in a more objective or factual account? If you are writing mostly essay, where might you bring in the personal side with an anecdote, either from your own life or from the life of someone connected to your subject? Finally, consider your audience and your purpose for writing the essay or memoir. Have you achieved your purpose? Will your audience get everything you want them to understand? Since creative nonfiction is often personal, it can be extremely helpful to have someone who is unfamiliar with the subject read your piece. They can tell you what they understood and what isn't clear to someone who wasn't there or doesn't know or even care much about the subject.

✒ Writing Journal Exercises

1. Write a personal reflection in the form of either memoir or personal essay. Begin with a moment in time and tell the story of that moment in detail. It might be a moment you remember or it might be based on research: go out and observe an event or activity. Try to capture the feeling you had (or have) at the time. Tell it as story (memoir) or as part of an essay. Combine scenic description and personal reflection.
2. Observe a social event such as a music concert, a pageant, a nightclub scene, a church service, etc. Describe the scene in detail. Notice the different groups that form within the larger group or the movement of people between groups. Notice people's dress or the way they interact with one another. Look for the little details that bring significance to the event or cause you to see it differently. Write down your description along with your reflections of this event.
3. Recall a moment from your childhood or young adulthood. Write down as carefully as you can all of the details you remember about that moment. Fill in the details as necessary with invented ones that fit the emotional truth of the moment. Invent dialogue, if there may have been dialogue. Write as accurately as possible, but allow for some invention. Allow some reflection on why that moment is important to you.
4. Find a newspaper article or a TV news story and read about a recent event. Research other accounts of the same event. If it is local, you may even be able to interview someone involved. Once you've gathered as much information as you can about the event, try to dramatize it.

Write it out as a story or a scene from a play. Invent the necessary details that will bring the situation to life.

5. Write a description of a place you have visited. Try to remember as many sensory details as you can about that place. What sights, smells, tastes, etc. bring the experience back to you? Why did you go there or how did going to that place change you? Include personal reflection on the place as you tell the story of your visit. Your description may become more story or more reflection.

6. Find family photographs and write about the memories associated with them. If the photographs are from before you were born, then interview people who still have some recollection of them. Write the story of the photograph, both what happens in it and what came before or after. Try to stay as close to the truth as possible, but invent the details necessary to bring the photograph to life.

7. Find a recipe for a food that we typically don't eat or don't prepare from scratch anymore. If you don't have a recipe, interview a family member or friend who used to cook this dish. Find out how the food was prepared, including as many sensory details as you can. Describe the kitchen it would have been cooked in or the smells or sounds of cooking. Allow yourself to reflect on why we no longer make this from scratch (as often).

8. Go to a store and describe what you see. Don't focus only on the products. Look for the security system or describe the lives of the cashiers. Observe the customers and the way they behave toward each other or toward the store's employees. Write down your description and your reflections on the experience. If you like, you can tell it as a story, following one customer. Or you might tell it as an essay with only brief scenes illustrating the details you want to reflect upon.

9. Write a braided essay. Choose any topic and write your personal history with it. What made you interested in the subject (or what makes you dislike it so much you have to write about it)? Then research the objective, historical or scientific perspective. Interview someone else about the topic or learn the history of someone who first did or studied the thing you're writing about. Write a page or two on each of these subjects, then cut up each passage into two to four pieces, fragments of narrative, bits of data, etc. Finally, weave these strands together in an intricate pattern to create the final essay, leaving out what you don't need and filling in the gaps with transitions if necessary.

11

Poetry

What Is Poetry?

Though we've been talking about poetry for several chapters, and though I've even asked you to write poetry, we haven't formally considered what makes something a poem. One reason I have been able to do this is that I expect you all have some ideas already about what makes a poem. That can be both good and bad. In the previous chapters, I've tried to work with those received notions at times and to challenge them at other times. Much of what we learn about poetry in our early school years (and, for that matter, even in undergraduate literature classes) can seem outdated or even archaic when compared to the poems we read in current literary magazines or anthologies. You may find contemporary poetry unfamiliar, even confusing. That doesn't make one form of poetry right and the other forms wrong, but students often come to an introductory creative writing class with a fairly limited idea of what constitutes a poem and with a fairly limited experience of reading poetry. Though that is perfectly understandable, now is the time to begin to expand our notion of what makes something a poem.

The Modernist poet Ezra Pound, who helped define poetry in the early twentieth century, came up with several definitions that are worth considering. One way to look at it came from an Italian/German dictionary, in which he noticed the following translation for poetry: "*Dichtung* = *condensare.*" The word for poetry in German literally means "to condense." From this translation, he took the insight that poetry is condensed or concentrated language, hence one of his dictums to "Use no unnecessary word." It helps to know that he was arguing against a kind of loose formalism of late-nineteenth-century English and American Symbolism— the French Symbolists are very different, and Pound admired their use of sound and image. Pound was especially adamant about the overuse of adjectives and adverbs and against filling out a line to fit a predetermined meter. He was one of the early advocates of *free verse* in English, though he also worked with and translated established verse forms.

Another way to define what makes something a poem (besides calling it concentrated language) comes from the linguist Roman Jakobson, who in his essays identifies six functions of language. We don't necessarily need to go into all of them, but we should note that, in Jakobson's theory, every speech act uses all six functions of language, though the emphasis may be more on one or another. A speech act has three elements, the speaker, the message, and the receiver. When the focus is primarily on the speaker (I am calling attention to myself), then he called it the "expressive function" or the "emotive function." When the focus is primarily on the content of the message, on getting an idea across to the receiver, then he called it the "referential function." But when the focus is primarily on language itself, on the way the message is constructed, then he called it the "poetic function." Of course, poetry can also be referential or emotive or any of the other three functions, but we might say that in poetry more emphasis is placed on how something is said than on what is said or even who is saying it.

To combine these ideas, we might say that we know we are dealing in poetry when the language is condensed and patterned in such a way as to call attention to how something is said. Normally, I don't care whether the statements I make have a rhythm or whether the words I choose sound good together; all I care about is whether they mean what I want them to mean and get the message across clearly. In a poem, I pay attention to other aspects of language, not just meaning.

Back to Ezra Pound. He argued that poems work in three ways, which he called *phanopeoia, melopeoia*, and *logopoeia*: image, melody, and logic or argument. Pound founded the school of Imagism, and believed that poetry worked by casting an image or sensory perception on the reader's brain that caused a response in the reader. He thought of an image as an *emotional construct*, not merely a static image, but one that moved the reader. He believed in composition by the musical phrase, not, as he called traditional meter, by the metronome. Rhythm was important to Pound, as were the sounds of rhyme and assonance or consonance, but a strict adherence to an established meter or rhyme scheme was not. The logic or the thought of a poem, the connections between ideas, was the third aspect that he considered important.

Similarly, Roman Jakobson considered the main elements of poetry to be rhyme, meter, and grammar. With rhyme, Jakobson included both the traditional idea of rhyming words and the use of repetition of sounds, words, and even images within a poem. Meter, for Jakobson, included traditional meter from many different cultures (he explores English, French, Russian, etc.) as well as other means of creating rhythm. And grammar included both the sentence grammar and larger logical or rhetorical structures of the poem.

So we can say that poetry uses sound (rhyme and other sound techniques), repetition, rhythm, and syntax to structure language and create a concentrated message in which how the message is said becomes as important as what is being said. Many writers have tried to show a link between the sounds of a poem and the meaning that it expresses, and though an absolute answer has been elusive, it seems clear that sound and rhythm do affect the content of a poem, even if the way they do is fairly complicated.

The good news for students of poetry is that most poets aren't linguists, and they don't worry too much about how sound and meaning work together in a poem. Instead, they rely on their ear, on their intuition, and their experience from reading other poems, to tell when a line sounds right.

They may learn about metrical systems or they may learn the tools of rhyme, the same way that a musician may learn about scales and chord progressions, but ultimately if it doesn't sound right, it isn't done yet, and when it does sound right to the poet, then it is.

Formal Poetry

We already began to discuss some aspects of formal poetry back in Chapter 3, when we looked at sound and rhythm in language. We noted that poets often work with *true rhyme* (or *perfect rhyme*) or *off rhyme* (or *slant rhyme*), different terms for whether the vowel sounds in the rhyming syllables are a perfect match or are a little different, but still recognizable, and that a rhyme can repeat one or more syllables, usually rhyming stressed syllables and any subsequent unstressed syllables. We also noted that, besides rhyming whole syllables, writers use other repetition of sound like *assonance, consonance,* or *alliteration.*

In that chapter we weren't discussing poetry yet, so we didn't discuss where rhyme is used. Probably the most familiar placement of rhyme is called *end rhyme* and, as you might imagine, this occurs at the end of a line. End rhyme is where we get the idea of a *rhyme scheme,* the pattern of rhyme across a stanza or stanzas, usually marked with lower-case letters, such as the *abab cdcd efef gg* of the English sonnet. But the end of the line is not the only place for rhyme. Many poets work with *internal rhyme* as well, where rhyme words are placed within the line, sometimes in the same line, sometimes in adjacent lines. Often internal rhyme and end rhyme are used at the same time, though typically there is no internal rhyme scheme.

Used in conjunction with other sound techniques, such as alliteration, assonance, or consonance, rhyme can create a highly structured feel for the language. Rhyme can often become a problem, though, when end rhyme is used in isolation. If the only interesting sounds occur at the ends of the lines, those words take on too much weight in the poem. It might begin to sound like sing-song, or it might come across as ironic or childlike—all of which is well and good, if that's intentional, but if the intent is serious and the sound is childish, then sound and sense are not working together. Often good advice is to stop trying to rhyme and focus on other aspects of poetry first. Or the opposite may be true: rather than stopping to use rhyme, a poet may need to explore using rhyme more consistently throughout the line.

Along with rhyme, most traditional poets used meter. This is a formal system to work with the rhythm of a poem, and in English meter, it relies on counting stressed and unstressed syllables. To be honest, meter is difficult for many modern readers to hear, and it does take practice. One of the problems probably has to do with the names we use for meter, which come from Greek and can be difficult to remember. Additionally, it may not be hard to tell which syllables are stressed, but what about the unstressed syllables? I'd like to call them less-stressed, since if a syllable had no stress at all, then it would be silent. In fact, linguists identify a range of stress in language, and there are probably not just two levels. There are at least 3 or 4 levels of stress, and there may be as many as 10, depending on how sensitive your ear is.

So stress is relative. A syllable that has a medium amount of stress may appear to be stressed if it is surrounded by syllables with less stress. Or it may appear to be unstressed if the surrounding syllables have more stress. The range of stress in a line may also make a difference. It is easier to hear the rhythm if all the stressed syllables have a lot of stress and the unstressed syllables have very little, but in many sentences the syllables are mostly somewhere in the middle, so hearing the difference between slightly stressed and slightly unstressed can be a challenge. Nonetheless, with practice you can develop an ear for rhythm as well. And if all else fails, look a word up in the dictionary to see where the stressed syllables are supposed to fall.

Once you begin to hear the differences in stress across a line of poetry, then you can scan its meter. Here's where it gets really complicated and where the terms get challenging, since they all come from Greek. In fact, Greek worked with a quantitative meter, meaning that the differences in syllables were actually heard in the length of the syllable, not the stress. Some Romance languages are still more like that today, but English, being a Germanic language, uses accent or stress for meter, since there is more difference in stress than there is in length.

There are several types of metric feet (units). The most common foot for English poetry is the *iamb* (or the *iambic* foot), which is made up of one unstressed syllable, followed by a stressed syllable. Its opposite is the *trochee* (or *trochaic* foot), which has a stressed syllable, followed by an unstressed one. Both of those feet have two syllables per foot, but some feet have three. The anapest (anapestic foot) has two unstressed syllables followed by a stressed syllable; whereas the dactyl (dactylic foot) has one stressed syllable followed by two unstressed ones.

You might notice that all of these feet have one stress each. There is one exception, called a *spondee*. This foot is made up of two stressed syllables, so it's rare that you would find more than one spondee at a time. Its corollary is the *pyrrhic* foot, which has only two unstressed syllables. Finally, there is a foot that is used very rarely in English, called an *amphibrach*: one unstressed syllable followed by a stressed syllable and then another unstressed syllable.

Terms for Meter

Ascending Feet	Descending Feet	Static Feet
˘ ´	´ ˘	´ ´
invent	mildly	buzzword
iamb (iambic)	trochee (trochaic)	spondee (spondaic)
˘ ˘ ´	´ ˘ ˘	˘ ˘
intervene	merrily	
anapest (anapestic)	dactyl (dactylic)	pyrrhic (pyrrhic)
		˘ ´ ˘
		unhappy
		amphibrach (amphibrachic)

The other issue with meter is the length of the line, which is counted by the number of feet in a line. The most common meter in English is iambic pentameter, which means that the typical line has five iambic feet in it. Other terms for the length of a line are monometer (one foot), dimeter (two feet), trimeter (three feet), tetrameter (four feet), pentameter (five feet), hexameter (six feet), heptameter (seven feet), and octameter (eight feet). You could keep going if you knew the right prefixes, but lines longer than five or six feet are fairly rare in English verse. However, trimeter and tetrameter lines are common in many forms.

One thing to note about meter, though, is that it is rarely so regular as the name would imply. Often in a poem that is primarily iambic pentameter, there are variant feet. So the poem may even begin with a trochee, but settle into iambic feet shortly thereafter. Where there is a disturbing image, it may be accented with a spondee. Or an anapest might be thrown in here or there for variety (adding an unstressed syllable is much less noticeable than changing the order of stresses in a foot). A poem where every foot was an iamb would be good for inducing sleep, but a poem with some variation on the typical iambic foot allows for some tension in the rhythm that holds the reader's interest. Roman Jakobson calls this "frustration" because it frustrates the reader's (or listener's) expectation of a regular rhythm, yet he notes it can be highly successful when done at an appropriate moment.

Specific Forms

Traditional verse forms typically consist of a combination of rhyme and meter. For instance, *blank verse* is unrhymed verse in a consistent meter. Often this is unrhymed iambic pentameter, but it could just as easily be tetrameter or another length of line (or another type of foot). The *ballad* form describes the stanza, which is a quatrain (four lines) with one tetrameter line, followed by a trimeter line, then another tetrameter line, followed by a trimeter line. The rhyme scheme is *abab* (or sometimes *xaxa*, where "*x*" is unrhymed). A ballad is usually a narrative poem made up of many of these stanzas, and from stanza to stanza the rhyme sounds may change.

Other forms describe the whole poem, not just the stanza. For instance, the Italian sonnet, which in English is usually written in iambic pentameter (though it may be tetrameter or hexameter as long as the line length is consistent), has the following rhyme scheme: *abba abba cddc ee*. The octet (or octave, an eight-line stanza or section of the poem) is always *abba abba*. The sestet (the last six lines) can have a variable rhyme scheme with three rhymes. So it might end *cdecde, cdeedc,* or *ccddee,* etc. The choice is up to the poet and may depend on the logic of the poem. (Remember that sonnets have a logical turn or volta at the beginning of the sestet.) The English sonnet, on the other hand, has a different rhyme scheme. Rather than using envelope or enclosed rhyme of the Italian sonnet (*abba*), it uses alternating rhyme: *abab cdcd efef gg*. Other rhyme schemes have been put forward for the sonnet, which always has 14 lines, but those haven't caught on. For instance, Edmund Spencer developed his own pattern, but very few poets since have used it.

Some forms, like the *villanelle* or the *triolet*, repeat whole lines in addition to working with a rhyme scheme. Typically, a repeated line is indicated with a capital letter (sometimes with a number) in the rhyme scheme, and the words that rhyme with it have the same letter in lower case. A *villanelle*'s rhyme scheme is: *A1bA2 abA1 abA2 abA1 abA2 abA1A2*. Each stanza is a tercet (three lines) until the last, which is a quatrain (four lines). The first line (*A1*) and the last line (*A2*) of the first stanza are repeated as the last lines of subsequent stanzas (alternating *A1* and *A2*), which also rhyme with an *a* rhyme in the first line and a *b* rhyme in each second line. Often the best way to understand a form is to read some examples while looking at a description of the form. A good dictionary of verse forms can come in handy if you decide you want to work in traditional verse.

For those who don't want to rhyme, there are some forms that rely only on repetition (which isn't as easy as it sounds). The *sestina* is one such form. Each stanza has six lines, and each of these lines always ends with the same words, which repeat from stanza to stanza for six stanzas in an intricate pattern. If we number the repeating words of the first stanza *123456*, then the next stanza would use the same words, but in the following pattern: *615243*. The next stanza would have the pattern *364125*, and so forth. You might notice that each stanza takes the last word of the previous stanza as the final word of its first line, then uses the first final word as its second, then the fifth final word, then the second, then the fourth, and finally the third. By the time you complete the sixth stanza, you will have used each word in every possible combination of this pattern. Often the sestina ends with a three-line coda that uses all six words: three at the end of the lines and three in the middle, in any order. The challenge is to keep using the six words in new ways throughout the poem. Some poets allow themselves to vary the words (to use "two" instead of "to," for instance, or to change "bright" to "brightly"). Others don't modify the words, but use them in different locations in a sentence, perhaps using them as nouns in one place and verbs in another.

Alternatives to Meter

Like repetition can be an alternative to rhyme, there are alternatives to meter in verse. One of the suggestions I often have for students who have a hard time distinguishing stressed and unstressed syllables is to simply count the beats in a line. These might be the strongest stresses or any syllable that you hear as a stress. Working with a regular number of beats per line (or a pattern of beats in the lines of a stanza) can give your poetry a sense of structure and rhythm.

Anglo-Saxon verse typically did not use meter, but did have four strong stresses in a line, separated by a *caesura* or pause in the middle of the line. (In metrical poetry, the caesura is also important and is one of the ways to add some variation to the line.) Anglo-Saxon verse also did not rhyme, but did use alliteration in every line. While there's no law that you have to follow all the rules of Anglo-Saxon poetry, such as the *kenning*, a device of naming something by combining two words to describe it, you may want to borrow some of its features.

Other poets don't count stresses, but instead count syllables. In French and other Romance languages, the *alexandrine* line consists of 12 syllables. Modern poets have found their own, often elaborate patterns. A good example is Marianne Moore, whose stanzas usually follow a syllabic pattern that is unique to each poem.

Free Verse

Writers who choose not to use rhyme or meter or a recognized alternative are usually described as writing *free verse*, though many, even the early practitioners, have argued that free verse is anything but free. One way of describing the restrictions on free verse is to say that, rather than using a predetermined form, free verse uses a form that is organic. Organic form arises out of the content or is in a dynamic relationship with what is being said. A free verse poet doesn't use no form, but instead invents a new form for each poem that is adequate to the content at hand.

In other words, as with formal verse, free verse is structured language, but the structures aren't given. Free verse poets work with many of the same techniques that formal verse poets do, but they use them when they need them, not when a form demands. So a free verse poet may use irregular line lengths and irregular stanzas. Or a free verse poet may use lines of roughly the same length without counting metrical feet, but instead composing based on another sense of rhythm. Some free verse poets have been inspired by jazz or blues. Others have listened to other forms: Walt Whitman is often thought to have been influenced by Biblical language. Alan Ginsberg wrote his poem "Kaddish" based on the Jewish prayer. Free verse poets create *found poems* out of texts they have discovered in ordinary settings, using line breaks to highlight different aspects of the passage that weren't the original intent.

The use of lines to break up the language and emphasize how it is said more than what is said is part and parcel of all poetry, yet with free verse, the poet has more liberty in how to break up the poem, and even whether to indent lines and set words or images next to each other.

Juxtaposition is one aspect of traditional verse that free verse relies on. Both free and formal verse rely on *enjambment*, which is breaking the line between words where there would normally not be a pause in a sentence. There is both strong enjambment, where you would be very unlikely to pause, and weak enjambment, where you don't need to pause, but pausing doesn't disrupt the sense or rhythm of the sentence.

Many free verse poets (and traditional verse poets) conceive of poetry as an oral art form, where the performance of the poem is as important as the form it takes on the page. Other poets have experimented with *concrete poetry*, poetry that is a combination of visual and verbal art. Some concrete poems take a recognizable shape, whereas others focus more on the spatial arrangement of words or letters in abstract shapes or patterns. The poem may be so visual that it is unreadable, or it may be something a reader can read aloud, yet the shape of the poem is also part of its meaning. Some concrete poets attempt to change the way we read, even printing a poem in such a way that there is no definite place to start. Rather than reading from the upper-left to the lower-right of the page, we are invited to choose a starting place in the poem and read in any order.

Naturally, the meaning we get from a text may be affected by the order in which we read it.

Free Verse Forms

Though none of the forms listed below are quite as prescriptive as the forms of traditional verse, they can give a poet some strategies for developing a poem or part of a poem. Here are a few you might try.

List poem: As the name suggests, this form of poem is made up of a list. Usually, the poem is not only a list of individual words (though some are structured that way), but uses repetition and variation to provide a kind of rhyme and rhythm to the poem. Often the poet will use *anaphora*, beginning each list element with the same word or phrase or varying part of it after a few repetitions, or use *epistrophe*, repeating the same word or phrase at the end. The length of each part of the list may vary from a word or two, to several phrases, or a poet may include a list within the list.

Question and answer poem: Like the list poem, the name describes the form. Some poets will begin the poem with a list of questions and end it with answers in the same or in reverse order. Other poets will alternate questions and answers. The answers may or may not answer the questions directly. Sometimes the answers seem tangential or misleading, yet are humorous or cause the reader to think twice about the question. As with the list poem, repetition (of the types of questions or of phrases in the answers) and variation, especially in the length of the questions or the length of the answers, add variety and tension to the poem.

Recognized forms: Almost any common form can be mined as a form for free verse poetry. Poets have used definitions, letters, job descriptions, personal ads, and many other common texts as models for their poems.

Prose poems: Another recognized form is the prose paragraph. Poets since Charles Baudelaire have experimented with using prose as poetry. Like all other poems, the *prose poem* uses concentrated language. It relies heavily on image (as does most free verse). Yet it also pays attention to the rhythms of prose and to the sounds of words, especially internal rhyme, assonance, consonance, and alliteration. Some poets describe the prose poem as poetry without lines; others call it one really long line of poetry.

How to Revise Poetry

Consider whether the current form is working well for you. If the poem is free verse, how would it work in blank verse or in a traditional form? If it is written in formal verse, then consider whether a freer form would be beneficial. Look for more words that repeat the sound of important words, whether that is through rhyme or other sound techniques. Consider making end rhyme into internal rhyme by changing the line endings. Or look for other places where you could repeat a word or phrase, perhaps with some variation.

Consider the length and indentation of your lines. Avoid centering poems, at least until they are nearly finished. It is easier to see the relative balance of two lines if they aren't centered—everything centered automatically looks even. Follow Ezra Pound's advice and cut any unnecessary words. Make the language as compact as possible and try to replace vague generalities with concrete and specific images that evoke feeling in the reader.

Read the poem aloud to yourself. You will quickly hear what doesn't sound good enough. Or try memorizing the poem. The parts that you just can't seem to memorize are probably the lines that need the most work. If that isn't enough, then try reading the poem in public. With an audience staring you down, you will quickly learn which lines are keepers and which ones are duds. If the energy in a line lags, then cut it out or add something to give it the energy it needs.

Consider the speaker of the poem. To whom is she or he speaking and why? What kind of language would he or she use? Is there an argument or a rhetorical structure to what the speaker would say? What is the speaker's emotional state and how would that affect what is said?

Consider the balance of the poem and whether the beginning or the end needs development or could be cut back. What did you need to get the poem started? Does your reader need that as well, or can the reader begin with one of the stanzas after stanza one. Does the poem end with a sense of closure? Should it? Reconsider line breaks and stanza breaks, and how the poem would sound if you said it in a different order or with different patterns.

In other words, if what you say in the poem is sincere; if you have not said too much or too little; if the language and the form you have used are vibrant and fresh at every turn; if the beginning is a surprise and the end a revelation—then you have a poem. But if not, then you may have a poem that still needs revision. Don't give up, but also don't be satisfied too easily.

✒ Writing Journal Exercises

1. Write at least 10 lines of a blank verse poem. They should be unrhymed iambic pentameter lines. You may use (and are encouraged to use) internal rhyme, assonance, consonance, or alliteration, but you should not use end rhyme. Your lines should have five feet and should be mostly iambic, though you may use variant feet at times, especially if you do it for effect.
2. Write a poem of at least 10 lines, using one of the free verse "forms" discussed in this chapter: the list poem, the question and answer poem, or a poem based on another recognizable kind of writing like a definition, a letter, or a job ad. Use repetition and variation to give your poem structure and tension.
3. Write a poem using one of the traditional verse forms discussed in this chapter: the sonnet, the villanelle, the ballad, or the sestina. Or find another formal verse poem to work with from a poetry dictionary.
4. Write a found poem. First find an interesting passage to work with. In its original context, it may not be all that interesting, but when you take it out of context and rearrange it as a poem, you can find some interest in it. The original should not be a poem. Instead, you are looking for a prose paragraph to work with. Then break this up into lines, possibly using indentation. Don't change the order of the words in the original passage, but instead use line breaks to highlight words or parts of words and to emphasize patterns in the original.
5. Translate the grammar of a poem. If you don't speak another language, you can take a poem that you have read and "translate" it by following the sentence patterns but changing the concepts. Replace each noun with another noun, and each verb with another verb, etc. For some little

words, like "a," "and," or "the" you might keep the original word, rather than trying to substitute. Write on a completely different subject, but follow the syntax of the original, in other words.

6. Write a concrete poem. Let the visual shape of the poem influence the content. Either write a poem in the shape of its subject or write a poem that doesn't go from left to right and top to bottom, but that is visually organized on the page to encourage the reader to enter it in one of several starting points.

is probably flash fiction. Fiction can be any length, but how you set about telling your story will depend on what length you are shooting for, and for the beginning short story writer, this is often one of the biggest challenges. If you are shooting for 7 to 15 pages (a reasonable length for a story, especially if you are also working on other genres), then you really only have room to develop a few scenes. Everything has to be focused around a few central moments, and you have to find a way to reveal essential background details that help us understand those moments without overburdening the story with a lot of scene.

A short story will likely involve two to three main characters with a supporting cast of maybe two to three more. In a novel, you might tell the story of two whole families and take time to develop each of those characters; in a story, you will focus on a couple of main characters and their closest relationships.

Time is also more limited in a short story than in a novel. A short story may take place in one scene that lasts an hour or less, or it may take place over the span of a few days. At least, the main time frame of the story will be fairly limited, though there are techniques to weave other times into the main narrative, as we shall discuss later.

The action of the short story is also very limited. Whereas a novel may tell the story of a character's life or one period in the character's life, a short story deals with a very specific series of events. The action of a story begins very soon, usually on the first page, with very little exposition. A novel may take an opening chapter or two to set the stage and only then introduce the initial conflict. In a short story, every action must be unified and related to the central conflict. There is no room for digression or for long exposition. The novelist can afford to be a little self-indulgent; the short story writer must be brutal in cutting any unnecessary detail.

Because we are more used to the longer form of the novel, it takes some adjustment to think in terms of the short story and the limitations it imposes. Framing the story, finding an appropriate beginning and end, can be a challenge. Often first drafts read more like the synopsis of a novel than like a short story. That is probably okay—the author needs to know the broader context of the character's life and then find the window on a short story within the broader picture. But you have to be willing to make those tough choices and jettison some of the juicy scenes you've written in order to tell the story as a short story and keep it focused. Never fear, though. Those good scenes may be the genesis of another story, and some writers even publish linked story cycles or novels in stories, if they are all centered on a character or a group of related characters.

Character and Setting

Despite the differences between longer forms and short fiction, there are many similarities, of course. Two of these are character and setting. As we said in the chapter on character, the motivations and desires of the characters drive the story. Without complex characters that are portrayed with some emotional depth, there isn't much to hold a reader's interest in a story. If characters are one-dimensional, then the plot of the story often feels contrived, but if the characters have depth and we see the plot develop from the interactions and motivations of its characters, we experience the story as real, even if the events are magical or out of this world.

Portraying well-rounded characters in short fiction is a challenge, though. In a novel, you have chapters in which to develop each character trait, and you can give a character's entire history if you wish. In a short story, there simply isn't time or space to show everything about the character's life and personality. It is likely that a few key traits will be explored in detail. At the same time, though, enough other personality traits need to be suggested with a few touches that the reader can intuit the full character. Finding the right touches and choosing where to slip them in can be a challenge. The short story writer is more of a minimalist, while the novelist can afford to be a maximalist. Nonetheless, character drives the story for most contemporary fiction.

However, characters can't exist in isolation. There has to be a stage for them to play on, a context in which the action unfolds. Setting is an equally important aspect of the story. Often we remember the details of place as well as or better than we remember details of character. Yet in writing a story, setting can be easy to overlook. We think about the actions we want the characters to do. We think about what they think or what they say, but we don't remember to put them somewhere or to deal with the limitations of that reality.

As with character, including setting in the short story can be a challenge. In a novel, there may be room for long descriptive passages. In a short story, any description is often brief and may even be fragmentary. The short story writer paints the picture with just a few brushstrokes, enough to suggest the scene, yet not so many that they slow down or overwhelm the action. As with character traits, the setting is often worked in with a few details here and there, along with the occasional descriptive paragraph. And fortunately, setting and character often go hand in hand, one suggesting the other.

Often the sensory perceptions of the setting that the characters notice will reveal a lot about their emotional state. If an author describes a room as cold and dank, the reader is likely to experience it in a negative way. If on the other hand, the same room were warm and cozy, the reader would likely have good associations. Setting can be used to suggest the mood of the characters, in other words, without the need for the author to tell the reader how the characters feel.

When the setting is an integral part of the story and something with which the characters interact, it is almost a character in its own right. Of course, the setting has no motivation unless it is personified (for instance, if a building comes alive in a horror story or surrealist story).

Nonetheless, it can exert an influence on the characters or can present obstacles that the characters must overcome. The weather often functions this way, but so can a flood or fire or any other part of the setting that might shift or change.

The perspective used to show the setting can also have an effect on the mood or the character of the setting. As we discussed in the chapter on perspective and point of view, a close-up perspective may give one perception of a place, while a panoramic view may give a completely different one. Both the amount of information portrayed and the emotional impact change depending on the angle of vision. An unusual perspective in description can lead to a disoriented feeling in the story.

Similarly, the choice of narrator makes an enormous impact on the tone and voice of the story. The amount of information that the narrator knows as well as her or his bias affects how the reader judges the events of the story, yet the author has other ways of getting some information across to the reader so that the narrator's perspective might be called into question, if desired.

Scene

The most basic unit of short fiction is the *scene*. We often think of the story in terms of a sequence of scenes, and indeed, a story may consist of one extended scene or it may be a series of related scenes. A scene is a passage in the story where the focus of the writer (or the narrator and the reader) slows down and follows the action as it happens. We get more detailed descriptions in a scene. We have many sensory images, the characters are set in action, and there may be dialogue.

In many ways, the scene functions like a story in and of itself, which is why some stories can be only one scene long. The scene follows the pattern of the narrative arc, though if it is not the opening scene, there is less need for exposition, and if it is not the concluding scene, then the crisis for the scene will be less intense than the final crisis in the story and the resolutions will be partial.

Nonetheless, most scenes begin with at least some *exposition*. This may be a word or a whole paragraph that sets the stage or establishes the time or the voice of a speaker. Occasionally, a scene may begin with action or dialogue and then fill in with some exposition, but usually there is something first to orient the reader in time and place. Pretty soon, though, some conflict or tension is introduced. As with any story, some complications happen—someone enters the scene or a new issue is introduced in dialogue—so that the end result of the scene is not quite what was expected at the outset. There will be some level of crisis and some level of resolution, though for scenes in the middle of the story the resolution may only be the introduction of a new tension that will be taken up in the next scene.

Characters act in the scene. They do things with one another, they come into conflict, or they move from place to place. But more importantly, in every scene something changes. If there is no change in the motivations or the status of the characters, then there is no real need for a scene. The relationships between characters or the level of tension should be different by the end of the scene. The story should be taken to a new level, in other words. Especially in a short story, there is little room for a scene if it doesn't develop character, establish the setting, and advance the story's plot.

Dialogue

Often the primary means of developing the tensions between characters is through *dialogue*. As you might expect, this is when characters talk to one another, yet for fiction, dialogue involves much more. In a first person or limited third person narrative, for instance, dialogue is the only place that a reader hears the thoughts and feelings of characters other than the main character. As we have noted, the *diction* a character uses tells a lot about who they are and also their emotional state at the time. Characters usually don't tell us their thoughts in dialogue, in other words, since that wouldn't sound natural in most instances. Instead, they respond to each other and address each other as they would in real life. Readers read between the lines and interpret the *subtext* of the dialogue in the same way we would in a normal conversation.

However, in a normal conversation, we receive all kinds of subtle cues. We see the gestures or body language that a person uses, and we hear that person's tone of voice. In fiction, very little of that is available to the reader, unless it is described as part of the scene, and writers generally try not to overdo it. If every line of dialogue is punctuated with an adverb ("he said angrily"), it starts to sound monotonous. If every line of dialogue is accompanied by a gesture ("she argued, waving her fork for emphasis"), it becomes ludicrous. Slipping in the occasional adverb or gesture is perfectly fine, if it can be done subtly, but writers have to develop other strategies to hint at the subtext.

One way to get someone's speech pattern across to the reader is with the attribution. The typical advice is to simply use "he said/she said" or some variation. As with adverbs or gestures, it may be okay to occasionally substitute another verb in place of "said," though this should be done sparingly, and only when the quoted dialogue itself doesn't adequately express the emotional content of the line. Most of the time, the best advice is to let the words do the talking and keep attribution to a minimum, sometimes leaving it out altogether if the speakers in an exchange won't be confused. If two people are talking quickly back and forth, then simply alternating their dialogue may be enough. Adding "he said" creates a bit of a pause and slows the reader down.

Adding the attribution to the middle of a long line of dialogue can add a pause or alter the emphasis of the speech:

"There, there," she said, after adjusting the pillow and turning on the night light, "now everything is okay and you can get back to sleep."

As we can see, the writer can insert some description within the dialogue to affect the pacing and tone. As with any technique, though, it is best not to overdo it.

When writing dialogue, you should follow a few conventions to help the reader identify who is speaking. Each time there is a new speaker, you should start a new paragraph, and always indent the first line of paragraphs in fiction. Similarly, a new topic or a pause in the conversation ought to be indicated with a new paragraph. You should usually indicate who is speaking unless it is clear from the context, yet you usually want the attributions to be as subtle as possible. And once the speakers are established, you may be able to avoid any attribution.

Yet these are just the mechanics, the basics of writing good dialogue. Besides knowing how to format dialogue on the page, you also need to know what to say in good dialogue. Though the common advice is that you want dialogue to sound natural, the reality is that good dialogue is far from normal speech. We are rarely eloquent when we talk, for instance, yet literary characters often use language extremely well, even if they use ordinary words. In real conversation, we beat about the bush, evade the topic, make small talk, and generally are poor communicators. Literary dialogue tends to get straight to the point without all of the chitchat (or with a minimum of it).

Yet literary dialogue can take advantage of some aspects of ordinary speech as well.

Because of the demands of short fiction (and even a novel) to keep the tension going at all times, there is little time for greetings or small talk. Characters confront each other much more directly in a story than they might in real life. I like to think of it this way. In a story, an author only reports what is absolutely essential. Every day your characters probably brush their teeth, take a shower, get dressed, eat, etc., yet we are told about those actions only if something important happens at the time, or if we may learn about them vicariously by finding out what the character is wearing, for instance (we assume that they put those clothes on at some point). The same is true in dialogue. We assume that there was chitchat. We assume that when characters enter a room they greet one another, but the scene may start after the characters enter and the narrator might skip over all the small talk. We assume that characters hem and haw and beat around the bush, but a little of that in dialogue goes a long way. The natural dialogue reported in a story is only the essential speech. A lot must be left out.

To make up for what is omitted, the level of tension in the dialogue is heightened. We tell a scene because it is the moment when what has been unsaid is finally blurted out. In dialogue, characters often speak out loud what they might only be thinking in real life. Or the other party in the dialogue reads between the lines and responds, not to what the other character said, but to what was implied (or only half implied). Writers can make use of natural miscommunication to up the tension in the scene. Dialogue can move more quickly when the characters second-guess one another and respond to what they think is being said. Characters contradict each other, they argue, or they argue without quite acknowledging the argument.

Every line of dialogue, if it is to be successful, has to do at least two things at once. It has to represent the character who is speaking and it has to advance the plot. Eudora Welty, in a *Paris Review* interview, complicates the matter even more, saying:

> Sometimes I needed to make a speech do three or four or five things at once—reveal what the character said but also what he thought he said, what he hid, what others were going to think he meant, and what they misunderstood, and so forth—all in his single speech. And the speech would have to keep the essence of this one character, his whole particular outlook in concentrated form.

So how do you learn to juggle so many balls at once when writing good dialogue? The best advice is to listen. Listen to the people around you. Borrow their language, hear how they speak, and then make judicious use of that language. Pay attention to the dialogue when reading fiction. See how other writers do it. The other best advice is to practice.

It will take time and lots and lots of revision to get it right, so expect that. Write scenes of dialogue in your journal, even if you don't know what story they will be part of. Try writing a scene of dialogue several ways. Give your writing to readers you trust and find out how they respond. Good dialogue has much in common with poetry or drama, so read your dialogue aloud. Listen for the rhythms. Listen for the dead weight of too much explanation. Listen for when the characters sound too much like the author. And then revise. Cut out anything that isn't absolutely necessary. Cut to the chase. And let your characters say what's on their mind or what they only are beginning to realize is on their mind.

Integrate the dialogue with the rest of the scene by weaving in some description and action. Don't allow the background to fade away for a page or more while characters talk, but let the characters be aware of their surroundings, and let the narrator remind us periodically that they are flesh and blood characters, acting in a space and responding to the things and people in that space. Your characters need to be more than talking heads in passages of dialogue, though often it only takes a few brush-strokes to paint the backdrop when the main focus is on dialogue.

Half-Scene and Narration

Between scenes, writers often include some *narration*. This isn't required, but it can help the reader navigate from scene to scene. Narration is the summary of events in the story. Time in narration is sped up. We may experience a period of hours or days or months in a single paragraph. The writer may tell the reader the kinds of things that would happen during this time, but does not describe any of the actions in a specific moment. The narrator may also comment on the events of the story in narration, weighing the import of the events that have transpired or revealing important details that affect the way we view the scene that just occurred or the one that is about to happen.

You might say that in narration, nothing happens. It is a way to advance time and fill in some details. It extends the status quo of the previous scene until the next moment when something disrupts the status quo, leading to a new scene and new story development. Yet a lot can be done in narration. Character development often comes across in passages of narration. The character's everyday routine may be established (so it can be disrupted later). The setting can be described, a new broader perspective can be given to events: if scene is the close-up of fiction, then narration is the panoramic view.

Halfway between scene and narration is what we sometimes call the *half-scene*. If a scene involves action, developing tension, crisis, and resolution, the half-scene involves only a little, usually a bit of action or a line or two of dialogue. A scene advances the plot, but a half-scene does not. There is no crisis or resolution, since tension isn't allowed to develop. Yet a half-scene does have some advantages over narration. Because it dips for a moment into the level of concrete image and detail of the scene, the half-scene can be useful to show character or to set up the tensions of a subsequent scene. Often a half-scene involves a brief moment of dialogue, so that the information a reader needs can be presented in the character's voice, and we realize the character's knowledge as well as the way they respond.

When a scene doesn't seem to be going anywhere, yet there are lines of dialogue you don't want to miss, you may want to consider including them as a half-scene. Cut back dramatically on the scenic detail and present only what is absolutely vital. Fill in the rest with narration and only show that brief moment when something interesting was said or when an action took place, but don't belabor the moment by trying to make a scene out of a moment when nothing changes.

The half-scene is also a welcome relief in long passages of narration. It reminds us of the specificity of character and place. It can help with the pacing of narration and keep the language of a story lively and interesting. By balancing scene, half-scene, and narration, a writer manages the structure of the story.

Fable and Plot

The linguist and literary scholar Tsvetan Todorov and other Russian formalists use the terms *fable* and *plot* to understand the structure of a narrative. It can be a useful distinction for fiction writers as well. *Fable* indicates the chronological sequence of events as it happens in a story from the first moment to the last. *Plot*, on the other hand, refers to the order in which these events are revealed in the story.

Though we might think these are essentially the same thing, often that is not the case. Take, for instance, a murder mystery. In a typical detective story, the fable would begin when the criminal first realizes his motive. Then he plans the crime and commits it. But the *plot* only begins once the crime is discovered. The detective is confronted with a crime and has to uncover the events that led to the crime. She has to reveal the possible motives of the characters, determine who had access to the murder weapon, etc., essentially working backwards through the fable to the beginning. When all of the events that led to the crime have been uncovered and the criminal has been captured, then the plot is over and order is restored to the world.

Other stories may have different structures. The plot and the fable may run concurrently, as in the typical thriller, where the focus is not on a crime that has been committed, but on one that is about to happen. We may follow the main character as he tries to uncover who is after him and attempts to avoid getting framed for a crime he didn't commit.

The point is that though a chronological approach is a common means of storytelling, it is not the only means. The epic, for instance, starts *in medias res*, in the middle of the action, and only later does the narrator fill in the background of the story and provide context.

Even in a chronological narrative structure, there is a difference between fable and plot. The fable includes everything that happens to the characters from the beginning to the end. The plot includes only what is revealed to the reader through scene. The choice an author makes of which scenes to include, of what is important enough to devote a scene to, determines our perspective on the story. In some ways, this choice is dictated by point of view (or the choice of the most effective point of view may be determined by the choices of plot), since a narrator can only tell about the scenes she or he has access to.

Fiction, in other words, is artifice. The events of a story, if told as pure fable, don't have much meaning. One of the first choices is where to begin the telling of the story, then which moments to include, and finally how to end. It is in the selection of a sequence of events to tell *as a story* that fiction creates its meaning. Often the early drafts of a story are where the writer explores the fable, and with revision the writer begins to discover the plot that best reveals its meaning.

Often we find that the best opening scene is actually several pages into the draft that we have started. There is nothing wrong with that. Stories typically don't get written down in the order in which they will appear in the final draft. But realize that the slow opening pages may be what it took you as a writer to conceptualize the story, whereas your reader needs to begin in the middle of the action and only later learn some of the information in the writer's initial opening. Similarly, the writer may write beyond the best ending: after all, how do you know the best ending until you've explored the story further? You may write scenes that don't add to the story. Be willing to cut those out or transform them to half-scenes or narration. Be willing to discover in the draft you have written the pattern and the structure that will portray the story the way you want.

Time Management

As suggested above, the beginning of the story is not always identical with the first events of the fable. In order to handle shifts in time within a narrative, writers use a number of techniques. We will begin with the most straightforward arrangement of a plot: chronological order.

If a plot consists of a selected sequence of scenes, it is obvious that time passes in between the moments when something changes in the story. As we have said, one way to handle the passage of time is with narration. If my scenes are arranged in chronological order, I may decide to have a paragraph or a few pages of narration that represent the passage of time. The longer the narration, the longer the span of time it will probably cover. Pacing a story may be done in part by timing the length of narration. Or the writer may simply indicate how much time has passed within the narration.

But there are times when the writer wants to skip forward through time without narrating what happened between scenes. This may give a more abrupt or harried feeling to the writing, whereas narration might feel more laid-back. It may be that a long expanse of time needs to be covered, so fast-forwarding to the next important scene may be the most efficient way to do it.

In cases like this, the writer will leave an extra space between paragraphs. This is called a *narrative break*. Often, to make it clear to a reader (and a typesetter) that the extra space is intentional, you type three number signs ("###") centered on the blank line. For many writers, this is optional, but it can be especially useful if the narrative break falls at the bottom or top of a page, where the extra space might not be noticeable.

A narrative break indicates a change in time, place, or perspective. The most common use is to advance forward in time, skipping over unimportant details, though it can also be used to move between two scenes taking place in different locations or to indicate a change of point of view when the narrator shifts from one character's perspective to another.

When changing time with a narrative break, the writer can go backwards as well as forwards. We think of the main chronology of the story as the *narrative present*. This starts with the first scene of the story and usually ends with the concluding scene. Anything that happened before the first scene would be in the *narrative past*, and anything that happens after the concluding scene of the story would be in the *narrative future*.

When a writer includes a scene from before the narrative present, we call this a *flashback*. If I have a character whose story is affected by a traumatic event witnessed when she was five, I may want to show that scene as a flashback in my story, which primarily concerns events from when she is in her teens or twenties. Though we often think of the flashback as a vivid memory, it isn't necessary to indicate that the character has been thinking of the past as we move between the past and the present in the narrative. Flashback has become such a common element of fiction that writers can insert one without much comment, maybe just a mention of the new time to orient the reader.

Flashbacks can be tempting, and it may be worth a warning not to overdo it. Moving around in time can be confusing for the reader. Including clear transitions as you move from time to time helps, and so does a consistent progression in time. Have a plan and a structure in mind, in other words. If you flash back and forth in time too much, the reader will lose track of the narrative present. On the other hand, if you flash back to the most distant past, then move forward in time, and finally end up in or sometime after the last scene from the narrative present, the reader will likely follow the progression. Or you might flash back a little at a time, regressing further back in time with each flashback, almost as if recovering repressed memories.

Not all information from the past has to be revealed in scenes, however. Much more common is to tell about the past within narration. In this case, we call it *backstory*, rather than flashback. As with the epic, it can be useful to start a short story in the middle of the action and then reveal just enough information about the past in backstory narration to understand the present without disrupting the forward flow of time in the narrative.

Even riskier than the flashback is the *flash-forward*. This technique is fairly uncommon, so readers are more likely to be confused by it, but there are times when a writer will want to reveal in scene what happens after the conclusion of the story. When this is told before we reach the conclusion, I would consider it flash-forward, and we would then return to the narrative present at some point before the conclusion. As you might guess, it gets even more complicated than flashback, in part because we think of flashback in terms of memory, which is fairly familiar, but flash-forward seems like predicting the future.

Yet this may depend on when the story is *told*, compared to when the events of the story *took place*. Imagine a removed first person narrator who tells a story of what happened in her youth. The main events of her story all took place in her twenties, but perhaps those events had some bearing on a scene that happened in her forties. If that scene from her forties is woven into the narrative of her life in her twenties, then it would be flash-forward. Of course, the other option would be to start the story in her forties, then flash back to the events of the twenties and finally return to the narrative present in her forties for the conclusion of the story. Or a novel might start in her twenties and tell everything chronologically, ending in the narrator's forties.

There is no one right sequence of events, of course. Some sequences will be easier to manage than others. Short story writers often have to find ways to condense time and weave scenes together so that the narrative doesn't stretch for hundreds of pages. Ending with one scene will make a different impact than ending with another. In our example above, ending in the narrator's forties would place more emphasis on those events than on the past story of her twenties, so the author may want to end with the climax in her twenties, but include a scene from later in life that throws a new light on those events. Or if that later scene is tacked on after the main concluding scene, then we might consider it an *epilogue*.

Since actually going ahead in time with a flash-forward is so disruptive to the narrative present, though, often information about the future is revealed in narration, rather than as a scene. It is probably easier to receive a little information about the future from a narrator who has access to that information than to transport ourselves to a scene in the future. I would probably call this technique *forward-story* in correlation with backstory. You might notice from the hyphens that neither flash-forward nor forward-story are as accepted or recognized as backstory and flash-back. Tread with caution!

The main point is that the best way to tell a story is not always in chronological order. A lot depends on the narrator telling the story, the kind of story that is being told, and the meaning the author wants to convey by arranging the story the way she or he does. Often these decisions cannot be made in the first draft. Once the story is on the page, though, it can be easier to find and re-evaluate its structure.

How to Revise a Short Story

Of course, the short answer would be to say that in order to revise a short story, you should work on everything covered in this chapter, plus the chapters on character and point of view (not to mention issues of language and place). Nonetheless, here are a few tips on how to start that process of revision that I have found helpful over the years.

Consider your characters. Which ones are most important to the story's conclusion? Are they well rounded enough to be believable (assuming you are working in a realist mode)? Are the other characters developed enough and only enough for their roles?

Consider the narrator. Often a change in narrative point of view is just what it takes to breathe life into a story that lacks energy. Whose perspective is the most interesting? Is that character the main character or a peripheral one? Should the character tell his or her own story or would a more objective third person be the better narrator? Often the answer is a question of voice. Can you write the story in the voice of one of the characters, and if so, does that give it more energy? Or does trying to write in a character's voice get in your way? Would a less personal, but more familiar, third person narrator who is closer to your own voice sound better or provide an interesting perspective? Is the narrator's voice consistent? Does it fit the narrator?

Consider the scenes. Which are the most important? Which show the most change in the characters and which advance the plot the most? Which have the most tension? Which are flat? Could the flat scenes be told more quickly and efficiently with narration, or do they need to be developed? Try adding a complication or allowing another character to enter the scene. Try upping the ante by having one of the characters really speak his or her mind. If developing the scene won't work, try cutting it back to the barest minimum and leaving it as a half-scene.

Consider the narration. What details from the narrative passages might be developed as a scene? Where might you have glossed over an important moment in summary that deserves to be shown with image, action, and dialogue? Is there a good balance between narration and scene in the story? Bear in mind that typically many more pages are devoted to scene than to narration. If you feel like there is too much narration, try cutting back.

Consider time management. Is it always clear (enough) to the reader when and where each scene takes place? Is there a pattern to flashback (or flash-forward)? When shifting in time, are there clear markers to orient the reader? Does shifting in time help the story by collapsing the narrative or highlighting relationships between events? If not, could you replace flashback with backstory in the narration?

Consider the structure. Try rearranging the scenes in a different order. You might print them on separate sheets of paper and then shuffle them, reading in different orders.

Consider whether the beginning is really the best beginning. Should you start telling the story closer to the conclusion? Or did you leave an important scene out before the beginning? Should that scene be placed in chronological order or inserted as a flashback?

Consider the ending. Did you write past the end in order to tie up all the loose ends of the story? Would the ending be more satisfying (or more disturbing) if you left some of those issues unresolved? Where does the story reach its new status quo? Are you there yet? Has enough change occurred, either for the main character or in the reader's or the other characters' perceptions of the main character?

Consider the story as a whole. Is it unified? Does it present interesting characters who are faced with compelling situations? Can the story be read as a metaphor or as an allegory of another situation? Or does it present a unique outlook on a group or an issue? Could you add another layer of meaning?

✒ Writing Journal Exercises

1. Write three to four pages of a story. Your pages should include at least one scene and some narration. We should begin to get a sense of the characters involved, but we should not have the whole story. Your passage may come from the beginning, middle, or end of the story. Give this passage to someone else to read and let them guess whether it should be in the beginning, middle, or end.

2. Write a piece of flash fiction (1,000 words or fewer) that suggests a story. There will be minimal scene and minimal dialogue, but there should be enough to show the conflict faced by a character and to suggest a resolution. Often in flash fiction, the resolution is far from complete, yet it should have a satisfying ending, even if that is tentative. It should reach an end-point, in other words, even if the ending is open-ended.

3. Find three to four stories that you like and look at the opening paragraph of each. Then copy the opening line or lines, but adapt them as the opening for a story you are working on. You might choose a different opening scene for each opening strategy: keep the sentence structure and tone of the original, but adapt it to fit the characters and actions of the story you are working on.

4. Write a brief scene that is all action and only a few lines of dialogue. Incorporate scenic description in the action and try to build the tension of the scene with the movements of the characters. The action does not have to be big (as in a car chase); it might be minimal (as in characters sitting, fidgeting, or moving about a room). Try to show silence through description or use non-verbal sound to indicate the silences in the dialogue.

5. Write a scene of mostly dialogue where two characters misunderstand and misinterpret each other. Allow their misunderstandings to reveal the true tensions between them. Keep the temperature to a simmer, not a boil. Don't let the characters shout, but instead keep the tensions contained and yet nearly ready to burst. Emotions might be anger, but they might be jealousy, love, pride, fear, etc.

6. Write a scene from your character's past. This should be a character from a story you are working on and the scene should take place at least a year before the events of your current story. The scene might become a flashback within your current story, if it's related, or it might become its own story. For now, don't worry about the connections to your story, just try to envision a moment in the life of your character from her or his past.

7. Write a scene from your character's future. This should be a character from a story you are working on and the scene should take place at least a year after the events of your current story. It may eventually be mentioned in your story in narrative as "forward-story" or even become a flash-forward scene, but it may also be the genesis of a new story or just inform the resolution of the current story. Try to imagine in detail what your character will be like and how they will act after the events of your story.

13

Drama

What Is Drama?

Drama is writing that is meant to be portrayed by live actors. In this book, we will focus on drama written for the stage, though in a broader context drama might also be written for the movies or television. Though those forms share many of the same features, there are also many conventions that are very different between the theater and cinema or television. Because the theater is the original form of drama and because it can be less complicated than the more technological forms of cinema and television, we will focus on it. Of course, the theater can be as complicated as other forms, but it's a little easier to strip it down to just the basics and still produce something that could be performed as a play.

When you write drama for the stage, you write a script rather than a story or a poem. The conventions of scriptwriting are different from the conventions of fiction or poetry (and the conventions of writing a screenplay or a television script are even more different). I will try to give a basic introduction to scriptwriting in this chapter, though there is much more to learn about writing plays.

What Makes Drama Different?

One of the main things you need to get your mind around, should you decide to write for the theater, is that writing drama is very different from writing fiction, even though both forms make use of story as the main structural element. The demands of drama can be instructive to the fiction writer or to the poet. There are advantages and disadvantages to the form—and many of the differences are neither better nor worse, but just different.

Drama exists on the stage, rather than on the page. In other words, the script of a play is not the final product; it is but a means to an end. The final product of the play only comes once the actors have memorized their lines and performed them before an audience. A poem or story is finished when the author says it's finished. It may be completed when someone reads it, but the reading of the text doesn't change it (much). Reading a story or a poem is an interpretive act by the reader, of course, but a play company has a much more integral part in interpretation and even creation, than does the reader.

Once a playwright writes the script, she hands it to a director, who then works with a cast and crew to create the finished product. Anyone who has been in a play knows that the director wields a lot of power with the script. She may cut lines or even whole scenes if she wishes. She might rewrite the lines, updating Shakespeare for a modern setting or recasting *A Doll's House* in ancient Rome. Even if she sticks fairly close to the original script, the director has to cast the play and make other decisions that affect the audience's experience dramatically.

In addition, each actor has enormous input into how the character looks, acts, and sounds. The interpretation of the lines begins with the script, but ends with the actor's performance. He may place more emphasis on one word than on another and thereby change the meaning of a line. He may walk briskly across the stage and give a different feeling to the scene, or he may speak rapidly or slowly and make a line funny or serious.

The stage is created by a set crew. A designer designs the space in which the actors act. This is based on the script, to be sure, but it is also limited by the budget for the production. And it can be enhanced by the artistic vision of the designer. The props manager finds the props and the costume designer creates the costumes. Since set, costumes, and props are all real things, they cost money or the effort to find someone willing to lend them.

In a story, I can easily give my character a huge diamond ring or a light saber. In a play, someone will have to create a ring that looks like a huge diamond or a prop that looks and acts like a light saber, which is a little more challenging on stage where special effects can be limited compared to in a movie. I can set my story in ancient Greece or on another planet. On stage, someone has to figure out how to transport the audience to this strange locale.

The main difference I'm getting at is that the theater is a collaborative act. The dramatist who writes the script is only one player in the action. Often in early productions, the script even gets modified by the company who produces it, usually in collaboration with the playwright. As a writer, you have to learn to give up control to write for the theater. The pay-off is that you have a lot of help to realize your vision.

Another difference between drama and fiction or poetry is that everything must happen on stage. This can be a huge advantage, since you have an actual person to deliver your lines. The actor can make a line of dialogue work in drama that would seem flat or unrealistic in a story. We believe in theatre what we might doubt in a story, since we see it happening before our eyes.

Yet this also presents a challenge. Everything must be portrayed. Nothing (or almost nothing) can be explained. Drama typically does not have a narrator, though there are notable exceptions where a narrator is a character in the play. Without a narrator, there is no one to tell us what happened, so we have to dramatize every moment. Similarly, the playwright can't reveal the characters' thoughts except through dialogue. Every action, every symbol, every piece of information must be visually or audibly manifest on the stage or revealed in dialogue.

Writing drama is a unique challenge, in other words, and perhaps the best advice is to be in a few plays before you start writing one! Acting or directing or working on the crew will give you more insight into how plays get made than any textbook could. And yet, even if you haven't acted or worked on a theater production, there is much that we can learn from considering and even attempting drama.

Conventions of the Play Script

Before we get into the actual writing of the play, it is probably best to consider a few conventions that are used for writing a script. Typically, the script begins with the *cast of characters*. This is a list of the names of the characters, followed by a brief description of each. Often this is the only place where the playwright tells the director what a character should look like or how he or she should behave. Sometimes these descriptions are fairly elaborate: a sentence or two. Other times, the playwright may give only a word or two of description, leaving the director to interpret the characters from the dialogue in the script, and giving the director leeway in casting.

Another form of instructions for the director and crew comes in the *stage directions*. Typically, at the outset of a new scene, the playwright will indicate what the stage should look like. Again, this can be an elaborate description of a paragraph or two, or it can be just a few words, such as: "A drawing room." These may be in italics at the beginning of a scene or between lines of dialogue, or often when they are included within the dialogue, they are set off by parentheses.

Stage directions within the dialogue often include notes to the actors that indicate what they should be doing. Naturally, when and where a character enters or exits will be indicated.

However, the playwright doesn't write out the actor's every move—much is left to the actors' and the director's interpretation. A director will usually give the actors their *blocking*, which may vary depending on the physical constraints of the set or the director's vision. What the playwright includes in the stage directions are the movements or actions that are important to the play. If the character needs to be seen waving a pistol around in scene 2, this will be in the stage directions. If a line needs to be delivered a certain way, this can also be included in stage directions, though usually this is reserved for when it is absolutely necessary.

Dialogue is written without using quotation marks in a play script. There are two conventions for how to format this. The normal format for a play manuscript (the typed version) is to center the character's name, then on the next line begin their lines of dialogue. Short stage directions can follow the name on the same line or longer stage directions can be on a line of their own. Between each character's lines, place a blank line.

In published play scripts, however, the convention is to put the character's name at the beginning of the line, followed by a colon, a space, and then all of the character's lines. Here, too, there is usually an extra line of space between each character's speech. The published format saves paper and probably looks more familiar to many readers, but the manuscript format is easier to follow on the stage. For your own use, you can use either format, or in a class, use the one your instructor prefers. If you plan to submit a script to an agent, you should always use the typed manuscript format, and be aware that there are more rules than are included here.

Typed Manuscript

```
                    Jenny (sobbing)
        Why are we always arguing with each other?


                         Todd
        We don't argue. We have spirited conversations!
```

Published Script

Jenny: (*sobbing*) Why are we always arguing with each other?

Todd: We don't argue. We have spirited conversations!

Dramatic Action

Since plays tend to be relatively short, you might think of one as a short story. A three-act play will usually last about an hour and a half, and the typical one-act play lasts about half an hour or less. There are also shorter forms, like the ten-minute play, which have become popular in recent years. When writing a one-act play or shorter, time and the number of scenes have to be very compressed. Even with a full-length play, the number of sets should be fairly limited for most productions, so there may not be many scenes or at least not many different locations.

Because the action is compressed, playwrights have held more or less to Aristotle's notion of unity, developed from Greek comedy and tragedy. Aristotle held that there should be three unities: the unity of time (the events of the play should occur on one day), the unity of place (they should occur in the same space), and the unity of action (they should all concern one central action or plot). As theater developed, companies challenged some of these notions, allowing the time of the play to span more than a day, for instance, but generally they have held to the basic principle. In order to keep all of the action in one place, Greek writers developed the convention of *exposition*. Violent and bloody scenes were typically not performed on stage, so a character would come on stage and tell the others about what had just occurred in another location. When violence was portrayed on stage, it was ritualized.

Even today, the amount of violence performed on stage in the theater is fairly limited. Though we have more elaborate make-up, stage blood, choreographed fights, and stage weapons, we still rely on actual violence much less in theater than we do in movies or on television. It's a lot harder to make a violent scene seem real to a live audience than it is on film. The playwright tends to suggest violence more than enact it.

And to keep the drama of the play condensed, playwrights often rely on the techniques of Greek drama to kick-start the action. A play often begins right after an *inciting incident* that happened right before scene 1. When the curtain rises, the characters reveal what this inciting incident was through exposition: dialogue about an event that has already occurred. Because the audience knows nothing about the characters, some information also has to be gotten across in the early dialogue. And yet, the dialogue still needs to seem natural, as if the characters would actually tell each other this information, so each character has to have a motivation to reveal any information in the exposition.

The action on stage begins, usually in the first scene, with the *point of attack*. This is when the central conflict is introduced and often the *protagonist* encounters the *antagonist*. Since the conflict of the play must be dramatized, usually the conflict happens between characters. Though the terms protagonist and antagonist suggest an adversarial relationship, this doesn't always mean that one is good and the other evil. Consider the classic love story. The protagonist may be the woman and the antagonist may be the man. Neither wants to be in love with the other, initially, and they may even spar verbally, until something brings them together to resolve their differences. Or if the lovers do initially recognize their attraction (say in *Romeo and Juliet*), then there must be another antagonist. This may be the fact that the families are feuding with one another, yet there will be a character, such as Tybalt, who plays the role of the antagonist.

Much like in fiction, the story will follow a narrative arc. Each scene presents us with a new complication (or complications) of the central conflict, and each scene should involve some change. Actors look for the changes in a scene: when the character's objective changes or when a new element is added to the mix, it is called a *beat*. Most scenes will be made up of several beats. A new beat may occur when a new character enters the scene, when new information is revealed, when the tone of the dialogue changes, or when a character achieves one objective. A scene may go from light-hearted to serious when the antagonist enters the stage. There may be conflict and then relief when one of the characters exits. A character's objective may be to get some information from another character, but once that information is obtained, the character's objective has to change. Possibly now it will be to find an excuse to exit the scene without revealing that she wanted that information. The changing objectives of the characters keep the action lively and hold the interest of the audience.

Like a poem or a short story, the play is usually highly structured. The props, the actions, and the dialogue all build toward the final climactic moment. Anton Chekov is credited with the principle that every element of the play (or story) must be necessary to the plot. If a gun is picked up in the first act, it ought to go off in the third (or at some point), but if it isn't going to be used, then it shouldn't be shown. And if it is going to go off in the third act, then it probably should be introduced earlier in the script so the audience realizes it could be important. Drama typically makes use of *foreshadowing*, in other words. A live audience may not accept the resolution to the conflict unless the elements of that resolution have been introduced already.

Some would argue that the most important elements of the plot ought to appear three times to reinforce their importance to the audience. Perhaps the gun might be mentioned once, then shown, and finally used. This is called the *rule of threes* and, though it isn't a hard and fast rule that can never be broken, it is not a bad principle to keep in mind. The playwright must always remember that the audience does not have the luxury of re-reading a passage that they didn't understand. A certain amount of reinforcement of the central images or concepts probably doesn't hurt.

As with any story, the action involves both the physical actions of the characters on stage and the emotional changes that they go through. The emotional side typically drives the physical. In other words, every physical action must be motivated by an emotional need. The playwright usually doesn't spell this out in the script, but it should be implied. The actors should be given enough to work with in the dialogue that they can create believable characters.

Dramatic Dialogue

Like dialogue in fiction or the language in a poem, dialogue in a play needs to work on multiple levels. It is like a poem in that it is spoken aloud and responds to a specific situation. It is like dialogue in fiction in that it reveals a lot about the character both by what is said and by how it is said. Stage dialogue is typically highly charged, in other words, maybe even more highly charged than in fiction because it also has to fill the role of the narrator. And yet that dialogue has to be spoken by a character and sound natural within the situation.

To keep the tensions of the scene alive, characters often disagree with one another or misunderstand what the other has said. This can allow for an explanation and present an opportunity for exposition, yet it can also allow characters to outdo each other in dialogue, playing out the struggle for power in a scene on the verbal plane rather than through physical conflict. Characters contradict each other, deny each other, lie, or tell the truth, all to try to gain a certain advantage over the other, whether they are conscious of it or not. And all the while, since an actor has to speak the lines, they should be relatively easy to say and sound memorable, like a poem. A playwright must pay attention to rhythm and sound, even if the play isn't written in verse, in other words.

The playwright may indicate that the characters speak over each other's lines or interrupt each other. And the playwright may take advantage of silence (especially if there is action) to create tension. The language should sound like natural conversation arising from the tensions and motivations of the moment, yet it needs to be structured like a poem or like good dialogue in fiction. The playwright can rely on the director to interpret the lines and choreograph the scene, and on the actors to make the language come alive, yet the playwright still has to give them realistic, interesting dialogue to work with.

On the other hand, dramatic conventions do allow for a certain amount of freedom from realistic dialogue. As in fiction, characters are more likely to speak their minds than in real life.

Characters may also speak directly to the audience in an *aside*, which the other characters seemingly don't hear, or they may reveal their thoughts in a *soliloquy*, when they talk to themselves, essentially speaking aloud what they are thinking, usually when there are no other characters present or when the action of the scene is frozen momentarily. Occasionally, a playwright will make use of *voiceover* to allow the recorded (or off-stage) voice of the character to be played through the sound system. Sometimes even a narrator's voice is heard in voiceover.

Because theater is live performance, dialogue can also be used in combination with the action. When a character says one thing and does another, this is called a *stage lie*. The character might tell another character he's throwing her letter away, yet quietly slip the letter in his pocket and tear up another sheet of paper instead, for instance. The audience sees that the character is lying, but the other character doesn't.

Similarly, the audience sometimes knows more than the characters do. If, for instance, an important fact is revealed in one scene, and then two characters discuss that fact in the next scene, but they are unaware of what has just transpired, we would call that *dramatic irony*. A playwright can make use of these techniques to heighten the tension in the dialogue. In each case, the dialogue and the staging of the action work together to create more tension.

Since the dialogue is the main element of the play script, it obviously receives the most attention. Nearly everything the actors learn about their characters comes from the dialogue. Most playwrights make minimal use of stage directions to indicate only the essential actions. Everything else is either alluded to in the dialogue or invented by the actors and director to go along with the dialogue.

Styles of Drama

So far, I have described drama in terms of realism. For instance, I have said that your characters should sound natural and that the set should be believable. Of course, as is true with fiction, in the twentieth century many playwrights began to work in styles other than realism. Plays might be surreal or they might be abstract. Characters may represent people we can recognize (whether contemporary or historical) or they may be types or symbols. The action of the play may be realistic or it may be symbolic. The characters may be more like characters in a dream or a fairy tale.

The set may be presented with varying degrees of realism as well. Perhaps it has a full range of props to suggest an actual drawing room or other space. Or it may just as easily have a minimalist set. Maybe there are only a few chairs, and the audience is asked to imagine the rest. The stage may be black and the actors may create a sense of place through their movement and the dialogue. Or the set may be symbolic, as in the play *Happy Days* by Samuel Beckett, where the main character is buried up to her middle in a large pile of earth.

The characters may also act as if they are really in the moment portrayed in the scene, or they may be aware that they are in a play. They may address the audience and even engage the audience in the action. Or they may address the author of the play and challenge their role as characters.

Most young playwrights start out writing more realist theater and only gravitate toward more experimental styles once they become familiar with the form. But there's no law that you have to approach it this way. If you want to incorporate some non-realist techniques, then why not give it a try? Or if you are uncomfortable writing long descriptions of the set and costumes then you may want to try a more minimalist approach.

How to Revise a Play Script

Since drama is performed live in front of an audience, and the lines will be recited by actors, the advice for revising poetry may come in handy when revising a play script. Read the lines of dialogue with an ear to how they sound and how easily an actor would be able to say them. Your actors will thank you if the lines are memorable and not too hard to spit out, though some challenges may be all right!

Since drama usually tells a story, much of the advice for revising fiction can be useful as well. Consider your characters' motivation and consider the narrative arc of the play. Do tensions develop over the course of the play? Are they resolved (enough) by the end?

Also consider practical issues for producing the play. How many different locations are there? Could you reduce the number of sets needed by combining scenes or using exposition in dialogue to get the essential information across without using a scene? Could you suggest some locations through lighting, rather than using a complete set?

Naturally, if you are writing a script for a particular company, then you will likely bear their style of theater and their budgetary needs in mind. If you are writing for any theater, then you may want to consider the kind of group who might put on your play. Is it something that might be performed in a one-act festival? Then you will likely want relatively minimal sets and costumes. Is it something for a church or civic group? Then you might use the kinds of props or sets they are likely to have on hand.

When revising the script, it can be helpful to have a few actors or friends give it a read-through. Though they won't memorize all of the lines in order to perform it, reading the parts in different voices and with some emotion can give you insight into what works well and what doesn't. Often a play script is revised extensively during the first production, so you may not feel you have a final version until it has been put on stage.

Lessons from Theater

Though I don't expect you to write a full-length play after one short chapter on drama, there is a lot that creative writers can learn by trying out the form and writing a scene, and if you are interested in theater, you might try writing a ten-minute or one-act play.

Fiction writers can learn a lot about the short story by examining the structure of a play. Starting the story in the middle of the action, after an inciting incident that gets the action going before the first scene, can be a good strategy. The use of exposition either in dialogue or in narration can develop character or explore backstory.

When writing a scene in a story, it is well worth visualizing it as drama. Thinking of the scene in terms of its beats, the moments in the scene when new information or the introduction of a new character or obstacle changes the objectives of the characters, can help sustain the tension of the scene. And thinking of dialogue as dramatized speech that reveals more than the character intends can lead to more highly charged exchanges.

Similarly, for the poet, thinking of the poem as dramatized speech that responds to a dramatic situation can help the poet find the voice of the poem. Thinking of the reader as another character in that dramatic scene can give the poet direction and focus.

Of course, fiction and poetry are not limited in quite the same ways that drama is, and drama is able to transcend the limits of the written text by bringing it to life with live actors and a physical set, costumes, and props. And playwrights have borrowed techniques from fiction, for instance by incorporating flashback scenes and even the occasional narrator as character.

♦ Writing Journal Exercises

1. Write a two-to-four page scene of drama using the published play script style (it saves space), which may be an original scene or one adapted from a short story you are working on. Your scene should begin with a

cast of two to three characters and some stage directions describing the set. It should include dialogue and at least two beats per character. Try to include a few longer monologues and some short exchanges.

2. Adapt a scene from a short story as drama. Describe the cast and the set as you would in a play script, then give the stage directions and dialogue. You may need to adapt the dialogue to get some of the narration across in the dramatized scene.

3. Write a realist dramatic scene. Describe the cast of characters for the scene and the set in detail, though you may leave some details open for interpretation by the director. Write dialogue that includes at least two beats per character and that sounds relatively natural, bearing in mind that dramatic dialogue often includes exposition.

4. Write a dramatic monologue for a character in a play. Begin with a cast of characters, set description, and a brief synopsis of the action of the play leading up to the monologue, then write two to three paragraphs in that character's voice. Consider whether you want the monologue addressed to another character or whether it is a soliloquy or aside.

5. Write an abstract dramatic scene. Your cast of characters may be unnamed human characters, such as a boy and a girl, or they may be representations of abstract concepts, such as Mr. Punctilious and Miss Passion. The set description may be very minimal, such as "a black stage with one chair," or it may be symbolic, such as "an empty field with a few cornstalks left standing" or "the top deck of a cruise ship." Feel free to make your dialogue more poetic or unnatural. Give each character at least two beats.

6. Take a scene from a story or the backdrop for a poem and describe it as you would in the set description for a play. If there are characters, describe them as you might in the cast of characters. Include some notes on their costumes or props.

7. Write a scene from real life. Take a situation you often encounter and describe the set and cast of characters. The set might be a simple description, such as "a school cafeteria." The cast of characters might be just the characters' names and one or two details about them. Write a brief scene that includes at least two beats for the important characters. Feel free to include other characters, even if they don't have speaking roles.

8. Write notes for how you might dramatize an issue that concerns you. You might give different sides of the issue to two characters or you might choose an allegorical approach, where the characters represent different qualities associated with the issue. You might write the script as dramatic dialogue or as a series of monologues where the characters don't interact but speak to the audience.

14

Other Genres

Are There Only Four Genres?

Arguably, the four genres we have been studying throughout this book are the main forms of creative writing. They have the longest history, stretching back hundreds and even thousands of years. Poetry goes back at least as far as there is written language, and oral poetry goes back even further, though it is impossible to know how far. Drama, often written in verse, goes back almost as far as poetry, and if you don't worry about whether it was written in prose or in verse, so does fiction. Our creation stories, myths, and epics are narratives that are at least as complex as the modern novel. And even creative nonfiction might be dated at least as far back as Hesiod's *Works and Days*, which combined myth with practical and poetic advice on farming and the rhythms of an agricultural life. Yet in the modern era, new technologies have given rise to new forms or at least new permutations of the old forms.

Cinema, Radio, and Television

One of the first technologies to arise and change the literary world in the late nineteenth century was the motion picture. Photography before that changed the way we looked at our world, but with the advent of the movies, we were suddenly able to tell a story with pictures and eventually with sound. Later, the technologies of video recording changed again when broadcast television came on the scene. Both forms draw a lot from the theater, but the camera lends itself to different kinds of scenes. In a movie, the subtlest emotions can be recorded by the camera in ways that are impossible on stage. The camera can take us to many more locations, and it can direct our eye much more precisely than is possible in a play, and yet the movies or television may not have the same emotional impact as live theater.

Writing for film or television presents a number of technical challenges, too. The format of a film script must be followed very precisely. This takes a lot of practice and good scriptwriting software, and as has been said before, it is beyond the scope of this book to go into every detail of writing for film. And yet, with the advent of small video recorders and even cell phones with video cameras, nearly anyone can now make their own short video. The production values may not be as high, and the script may not live up to professional standards, especially in terms of camera angles, transitions, lighting, and other directions for the script, but many an amateur videographer has tried her hand at a short film, a video collage to go with a poem, or a short documentary or video diary. Film may become more ubiquitous than fiction in the coming decades.

Similarly, the advent of radio brought theater to the airwaves. In a radio play, the sounds are the only important part. Besides the voices of the actors and a narrator, the radio theater audience was treated with sound effects that made the space and the action of the play come alive in the listener's mind. Though radio theater is much less prevalent in our world today, a twenty-first-century equivalent might be the podcast or audio book.

Graphic Fiction

Inspired by the new form of cinema, though also having roots in illustrated magazines, comic strips developed. These led to serial cartoons with both comedic and dramatic subjects. Strips were published first in newspapers and magazines; then comic books developed, which eventually led to the graphic novel, a serious literary treatment of the form. In comics and graphic novels, the concept of the frame is borrowed from cinema in the series of individual panels, where stylized visual art is combined with written text. Changes in camera angle suggest action, speech balloons represent dialogue, and thought bubbles reveal the characters' unspoken thoughts, bringing in aspects of drama. As in drama, nearly everything must be portrayed visually in the panel, though some strips make liberal use of the theater technique of voiceover, allowing some written text within the panel but not in a thought bubble to be associated with a narrator or using special effects lettering to portray sound-effects.

Though some graphic novelists do all the writing and all the illustrations, other writers collaborate with graphic artists. Graphic fiction combines elements of drama and cinema with the elements of fiction and the concise language of poetry. Though the model of the comic book is still the most common in this form, some novels have found other ways to incorporate visual representation of the scene, such as by combining cartoon panels with narrative passages or by using stick figure drawings within the text.

Kinetic Poetry

Technology has affected poets as well. The concrete poem was arguably a result of new technologies in printing, first with the printing press that made its reproduction possible, then with better printing presses and ultimately the typewriter and word processor that made it easier to arrange words and letters on the page esthetically. With the advent of computers and digital technologies, poets began to think of the concrete poem as more than just a static object. One of the goals of concrete poetry was to challenge the way we read. It isn't always clear where to start reading a concrete poem or where to end it. Setting the concrete poem in motion, or taking a regular poem and animating it to rearrange the words and form another poem, challenges the reader even more as meanings shift with the movement of the words and letters. Some kinetic poetry is controlled by a computer program—once you start it, the poem goes through a series of animations leading to the same final state.

Other kinetic poetry is more interactive, allowing the user choices or actions that will affect the final outcome.

Hypertext Fiction

Fiction writers have also experimented with computer technology. Even before the advent of the internet, some writers were theorizing about different structures for the novel, using cross-referenced footnotes or other techniques to allow the reader choices in how to read the text. Once linked hypertext became a possibility, some fiction writers gravitated to it to create a nonlinear story using linked text. The choice to follow a link or to continue reading the page you are on affects the story that a reader will see and the order that the reader will read it in, ultimately leading to a different reading experience and a different meaning depending on which paths the reader chooses to follow. Of course, as anyone who has read a hypertext story will probably tell you, the temptation to go back and re-read, following multiple paths and searching for the things you may have missed, is hard to ignore. Though so far the form has not taken off and is primarily relegated to the category of experimental literature, with the advent of e-books, the platform may finally have arrived that will make it a more viable and popular form.

Twaiku, TwitLit, and Social Media

Perhaps more than hypertext fiction or kinetic poetry, technology may be affecting the way we write through the way we use social media. Twaiku, essentially an adaptation of the haiku form to the 140 characters of a tweet, may seem to be the most obvious way creative writing has entered the world of social media. Writers have explored other ways to adapt poetry and fiction to Twitter by tweeting individual lines of poems, allowing collaborative composition across the platform, or writing stories composed in a tweet storm, a linked series of replies to an initial tweet. The ability to add images, animations, and even videos to a tweet has expanded the range of what can be done, incorporating elements of the graphic novel or even drama.

Other social media platforms such as Instagram or Facebook don't restrict the number of characters in a status update or post, and so can be used for a more extended project, yet they still offer the opportunity to share writing and to incorporate sound, video, or image. And the ability to link between posts or to link between social media platforms may be another way to make the hypertext story an accessible option. Not only do we have the ability to link on social media, but we are used to doing it, and we think nothing of clicking from a status update to a news article, then on to another. A live hypertext story on social media might have multiple entry points and multiple endings, which might then be taken in new directions through the likes and comments.

Maps and Games

Writers have even used features of Google Maps and other mapping platforms to create individual layers, adding memoir or story to the map in the tags they write for each place. Maps of fictional spaces can be created and filled with content that builds the story of that place. Or actual maps can be used to write a true or fictional story, allowing the reader to enter the story at any place on the map, and read it chronologically or geographically or in the order they choose. Links to other blogs, websites, or social media content can add layers to the mapped reality. And if extended reality ever becomes more than an experimental concept of overlaying a virtual reality onto a real environment, then the mapped story may leave the map and enter the world.

Other writers have entered the world of video gaming to create stories that the end-user controls by playing the game. Characters and characteristics of the setting are loaded into the program, but the actions of the characters are determined through gameplay, and the story is different every time it is played. When programming animation skills or the budget to implement them are lacking to create a full-fledged video game, writers have used the model of role-playing games to achieve similar ends in a low-tech environment. Some see this as a logical extension of the hypertext story, where the writer provides the materials but the user or reader creates his or her own meaning within the confines of the story.

Conclusions

Though it is fun and instructive to consider how technology is affecting the kinds of writing humans will do in the future or are doing today, it seems clear that technology primarily opens up new possibilities for writers to use the techniques we have been discussing in this book. It would take another whole book or class to fully explore how to write for cinema, television, electronic literature, etc., even as it will take many more books and more classes to fully explore the genres of creative nonfiction, poetry, fiction, and drama.

In this final chapter, my goal is to return our conversation to where we started. What strikes me about new forms of writing is how often they take elements of the four genres we've been studying and recombine them to create something new. This serves as a reminder that the genres are not distinct and separate things, but that all writers have always borrowed from one another and from other forms. The poet who never reads fiction or the novelist who doesn't try to understand a poem is seriously limited.

Paying attention to the sounds, rhythms, images, and sentence structure of poetry benefits the novelist or playwright as much as it does the poet. Understanding the structure of a story or the rhetorical moves of an essay benefits the poet as much as the novelist or essayist. And the hands-on practical limitations and sense of collaboration between writer, director, actors, crew, and audience found in drama are good for every writer to experience, reminding us that the written text is never finalized until someone reads it. Dialogue and performance can be found in any genre, whether this is the scene with actors on stage, the dramatized scenes of fiction or nonfiction, the speaker of the poem, or the performance poet.

This is one of the main reasons I am an advocate of the multi-genre introductory creative writing class. Not only have I found that some students come into a class thinking they will write one genre, only to leave it after realizing they are as talented or more talented in another, but I feel that we all need to learn from one another, and that the genres as we know them, though they will continue to exist, will also be recombined in new ways as creative writing continues to adapt in the twenty-first century.

✒ Writing Journal Exercises

1. Draw out a few panels of a cartoon in your Journal. Don't worry if your drawings aren't great; use stick figures if you need to. Vary the camera angle from close-up to panorama to suggest movement. Give each character speech balloons and thought bubbles for their dialogue or for their inner thoughts. Try to avoid using too much narration, but include sound effects and minimal narration as needed.
2. Think about the map of your town or a place you have been. Write descriptions for some of the locations on the map that might correspond to a story. They might be narration or they might include scenes with dialogue. Don't write much narration between the scenes, but write only what may have happened at that place at one time. The story may be true or fictional.
3. Try writing a poem or micro-story that is only 140 characters long. Or write a poem or story in a series of stanzas or paragraphs that are each 140 characters or fewer.
4. Write a poem or flash fiction to accompany a photo that you took. Try to keep the text brief. It can be longer than a tweet and shorter than your longest status update. Let the words play off the image but not describe it. Evoke a mood or tell a story.
5. Take your writing outside your journal by recording a voice memo or shooting a short video. If you don't work from a written text, then improvise. Give yourself and your actors a situation and film each other's interactions.

Appendix

Guidelines for Workshops

Procedure

1. Read the submitted work once to get a sense of the work as a whole.
2. Read the work a second time, annotating the margins with comments and questions.
3. At the bottom or on the back, write a substantial paragraph in which you give a general response and make suggestions for revision.

In workshop you will discuss each story or poem as a group. You should raise issues based on the comments you wrote in the margins. At the end of discussion, you will return your draft of the story or poem to the author, so you won't have to mention minute details, spelling errors, etc.

Some instructors ask the author to read from the work prior to discussion. Some ask the author to remain silent while their work is being discussed and ask the workshop to look to each other, not the author, for answers. Some engage the author in the discussion throughout, and some allow the author to comment after the workshop has finished their discussion.

Guidelines for Workshop Discussion

Be honest. If a story, scene, poem, image, character, etc. isn't interesting, you need to let the author know. Try to explain why it doesn't work for you in as much detail as you can. That will help the author locate the source of the problem.

Be gracious. Don't insult other writers or demean their intelligence or motives. You can often draw attention to problems by asking appropriate questions, rather than accusing or saying something is weak or wrong.

Be specific. Be as helpful as you can, marking problems in style and organization in the margins near where they occur. Let a writer know about mechanical problems, but don't feel obligated to identify or correct all of these items; correct grammar, spelling, and punctuation is the responsibility of the writer.

Don't just correct the writer's errors. It is much more helpful to both you and your colleagues if you try to pinpoint why a section is awkward, than if you simply reword it for them. If the only way to show what's wrong with a passage is to suggest another version, then put this in the form of a question.

When you can't be specific, explain your feelings or intuitions. A writer needs to know when a reader suspects something is not working or where he or she gets confused.

Look at the big picture. Respond to the ideas, shape, and strategy of the entire poem or story. Describe your overall impression; let the writer know what is working and what isn't.

Read the poem or story the author has written, not the one you would have written. Don't expect another writer to treat a subject the same way you would.

Always mention the strengths of the piece. Don't be stingy about praising good work. Even the roughest draft has some potential. Help the author find it.

Suggest a plan for revision. Let the writer know what you think the priorities for revision should be. What issues need to be addressed first? Which items are comparatively minor?

Guidelines for Receiving Criticism

Bring work to workshop when you are ready to receive criticism. It shouldn't be too fresh or too finished. You need to maintain a critical distance from your work and be willing to make changes.

Remember that people's comments are about the draft they read, not about you or about the poem or story you envision. Negative criticism only shows you have more work to do.

Where to Go from Here?

As I suggested in the previous chapter, many writers, after taking an introductory class, will want to take other university classes that focus on specific genres and go into more depth. The more you read and the more you write, the better your writing should become, and a classroom environment provides opportunities for feedback from your peers that can be hard to replicate elsewhere. So take advantage of the opportunities your program has to offer and develop the lasting friendships that will sustain your writing for years to come.

Many writers find a group of fellow writers and friends who can be good readers of their work when they're not in a writing class. Reading others' work in progress inspires the writer to continue on his or her own, and the feedback you get from trusted readers can be invaluable as you struggle to hone your writing. Having a writing group can help keep you writing and support you in your attempts to publish. You can celebrate each other's successes and console each other over the inevitable rejections.

Many writers will choose to continue their education after their undergraduate degree, pursuing a Master's in literature or another field, a Master's with a concentration in creative writing, or a Master's of Fine Arts in creative writing. Though the MFA is considered a terminal degree, the highest professional degree needed to teach at university level, some writers go on to earn a PhD.

No degree is absolutely necessary to become a published writer, and no degree can guarantee publication, yet further instruction in the craft can certainly help you on your way, and graduate programs allow an opportunity to focus on a writing career. The choice to go to graduate school is a personal one, and should be undertaken when you're ready to take full advantage of the experience. In the meantime, there are many things you can do to be more involved and more professional as a writer.

Summer workshops, weekend conferences, artists' retreats, local writers' groups, and online forums can support writing without earning academic credit. Many workshops and conferences include seminars or writing workshops with the same kind of feedback you find in a classroom setting, and typically the workshop leaders are published writers or literary agents.

Participants learn from the workshop and also develop valuable networking connections.

Literary Citizenship

Anyone who wants to be a writer owes it to themselves to become part of a wider literary community. Though some see the concept of literary citizenship as an obligation, I see it more in terms of opportunity. Sure, part of being a good literary citizen is to promote the work of others, but in doing this you promote literature as a platform and ultimately help to build the kind of environment that will lead to more success for your own work, and you develop friendships and networks along the way. Though the term may seem daunting, literary citizenship is easier than you think. Start with the things you can do now and set goals to do more when you can.

One of the easiest things anyone can do to be a good literary citizen is to buy books and read. That ought to seem like a no-brainer, but I can't tell you the number of people who say they want to be a writer and yet claim they don't like to read. Buying books is important, but if you aren't at a place where you can afford as many books as you want, then join your local library and borrow books. The more a book gets checked out, the more likely books like it will get ordered, so your library use leads to book sales. And if your library doesn't have the books you want, consider interlibrary loan. And if nothing else, you can spend time in a bookstore, buy a cup of coffee, browse the shelves and look at the books that seem interesting, and invite your friends along.

Don't stop at buying and reading books, though. Find ways to talk about them and help promote them. You might start or join a book club, or just talk about books with your friends, even if you don't have a formal group. You might post about books in social media or you might even write reviews of the books you read in online bookstores or social media for readers such as LibraryThing, GoodReads, or Litsy. A word of caution: many writers limit their reviews to the books they like and don't post negative reviews unless they can say something informative and somewhat positive. It's easy to develop a bad reputation for a few harsh reviews, and those can come back to haunt you. Everyone needs to find their own strategy for writing reviews of course, but if your goal is to promote the work you like, it may be wise to simply ignore the work you don't like.

Writing published reviews is a different matter. There, the in-depth nature of the review and the fact that your review is accepted by an editor helps to ensure a more even-handed approach. If a published reviewer has enough clout, she can safely pan a book if it's warranted, and the attention garnered by a negative review in a prominent journal may even be appreciated by the writer who's been panned.

Besides reading and writing about what you've read, new writers can gain exposure and promote literature by taking part in an open mic or reading series. If there isn't one in your town, you might even organize it. This doesn't have to be anything fancy or pretentious. Getting people out to enjoy good writing by local writers helps build an audience for literature, and maybe build your audience as well. Participating in a reading series can help you make connections that will lead to a personal writing group.

Consider getting involved with literacy groups in your community or volunteering at a local library or community center. Working with youth or with the elderly, helping to teach English in immigrant communities, or working with other marginalized groups can be rewarding and can promote a reading culture. You gain in experience as you develop networking skills that will serve you well when promoting a book.

Publishing

Since the goal of most writers is to be in print, you will eventually want to start publishing. It may not be too early to think about this if you've written some stories, essays, poems, or plays you're happy with. Though drama publishing is a little different, most writers get their start by publishing in literary magazines. And the best way to learn about magazines is to read them.

Fortunately, many have their full issues or at least a selection from past issues available online for free. Most serious writers will subscribe to some magazines or read the annual prize anthologies that are selected from the literary magazines.

Another step you can take before submitting to magazines is to learn everything you can about their submission guidelines. These can be found in the magazines themselves, on the magazines' websites, or in their calls for submission in *Poets and Writers, Writer's Digest, New Pages*, or services like *Submittable* or *Duotrope*. Make sure you format your submission according to the guidelines and make it is as clean and accurate as possible. Write a brief, professional cover letter, if the magazine allows, and always be professional in your correspondence.

When you do begin to publish, you should expect the submission process to take some time. Response times can be anywhere from a few weeks to several months. Some magazines may still take hard copy submission by mail, but many now accept submissions electronically, either by email or through a submission management service like Submittable.

You should also expect to receive many more rejection letters than acceptances, at least initially. Most magazines receive far more submissions than they could possibly use, so you shouldn't take rejection personally, even though it's hard not to. The best thing you can do to have the best chance of acceptance is to research your magazines carefully. Find the magazines that are most likely to want your work and find the times to submit when you'll have the greatest chance. Then you can only wait and hope and continue writing until you get a response.

Some magazines allow simultaneous submissions, so some writers submit the same piece to several magazines at a time, believing this will help them get published faster. Regardless of whether you submit to one place at a time or many, always be sure to keep good records of where your work has been sent and when you sent it. If you haven't heard anything within four months, it may be time to send a polite query to ask if it is still being considered. And if one magazine accepts your work, it is expected that you will allow it to publish your work and immediately notify any other magazines where it is being considered that you need to withdraw.

Magazine publication helps to generate an audience, which is one thing that book publishers will be looking for when you eventually try to publish a novel or collection of stories or poems.

Generating an audience on social media or demonstrating the network you've developed through literary citizenship can also help.

Research book publishers at least as much as magazines before trying to publish. Learn the differences between vanity presses, small publishers and big publishing houses. Most big houses only work with a literary agent, especially for novels, though poetry and short story collections are usually unagented. Small publishers are more likely to work with the author without an agent, but they will market your book and will pay royalties. Vanity presses or self-publishers expect the author to pay to be published, and the author is usually in charge of marketing and distribution.

Many poetry and short story collections and novellas are published through contests. Though there are many legitimate contests, there are also some well-known scams, so it is best to research a contest thoroughly before submitting. Avoid those with high reading fees or unknown judges. Some free contests will accept nearly anything that is submitted, and then make money by trying to sell you an expensive anthology, conference registration, or other related services.

Legitimate contests often charge a small fee, which may include a magazine subscription or a copy of the winning book.

Though the path to becoming a published writer may seem long and difficult, there are many things you can do now to take your first steps. Becoming a better literary citizen, reading books and literary magazines, and taking more classes are some of those. You can also explore further on your own with the resources listed below.

Resources

Creative Writing

Atwood, Margaret. Negotiating with the Dead: A Writer on Writing. Cambridge, UK: Cambridge University Press, 2002.

Bradbury, Ray. Zen in the Art of Writing. Santa Barbara, CA: Joshua Odell Editions, 1990.

Burke, Carol, and Molly Best Tinsley. The Creative Process. New York, NY: St. Martin's Press, 1993.

Burroway, Janet. Imaginative Writing: The Elements of Craft. Boston, MA: Longman, 2011.

Cameron, Julia. The Right to Write: An Invitation and Initiation into the Writing Life. New York, NY: Jeremy P. Tarcher/Putnam, 1998.

Dillard, Annie. The Writing Life. New York, NY: Harper & Row, 1989.

Goldberg, Natalie. Writing Down the Bones: Freeing the Writer Within. Boston, MA: Shambhala, 2005.

Lamott, Anne. Bird by Bird: Some Instructions on Writing and Life. New York, NY: Anchor Books, 1995.

Sellers, Heather. The Practice of Creative Writing: A Guide for Students. Boston, MA: Bedford/St. Martins, 2008.

Creative Writing Pedagogy

Beck, Heather. Teaching Creative Writing. Houndmills, Basingstoke, Hampshire, UK: Palgrave MacMillan, 2012.

Clark, Michael Dean, Trent Hergenrader, and Joseph Rein. Creative Writing in the Digital Age: Theory, Practice, and Pedagogy. London, UK: Bloomsbury Academic, 2015.

Leahy, Anna. Power and Identity in the Creative Writing Classroom: The Authority Project. Clevedon, UK: Multilingual Matters, 2005.

Ritter, Kelly, and Stephanie Vanderslice. Can It Really Be Taught?: Resisting Lore in Creative Writing Pedagogy. Portsmouth, NH: Boynton/Cook Heinemann, 2007.

Vanderslice, Stephanie. Rethinking Creative Writing in Higher Education: Programs and Practices that Work. Wicken, Ely, Cambridgeshire, UK: Professional and Higher Partnership, 2010.

Walker, Elaine. Teaching Creative Writing: Practical Approaches. Ely, Cambridgeshire, UK: Professional and Higher Partnership, 2012.

Fiction

Anderson, Linda, and Derek Neale. Writing Fiction. London, UK: Routledge, 2009.

Burroway, Janet, Elizabeth Stuckey-French, and Ned Stuckey-French. Writing Fiction: A Guide to Narrative Craft. Boston, MA: Longman, 2011.

Butler, Robert O., and Janet Burroway. From Where You Dream: The Process of Writing Fiction. New York, NY: Grove Press, 2005.

Cowan, Andrew. The Art of Writing Fiction. Harlow, UK: Longman, 2011.

Dufresne, John. The Lie That Tells a Truth: A Guide to Writing Fiction. New York, NY: W. W. Norton, 2003.

Forster, E. M. Aspects of the Novel. New York, NY: Harcourt, Brace & Company, 1927.

Gardner, John. The Art of Fiction: Notes on Craft for Young Writers. New York, NY: A. Knopf, 1984.

Grenville, Kate, and Sue Woolfe. Making Stories: How Ten Australian Novels Were Written. North Sydney, NSW: Allen & Unwin, 1993.

Kardos, Michael. The Art and Craft of Fiction: A Writer's Guide. Boston, MA: Bedford/St. Martin's, 2013.

Kundera, Milan, and Linda Asher. The Art of the Novel. London [u.a.]: Faber and Faber, 1988.

Le Guin, Ursula K. Steering the Craft: A Twenty-First Century Guide to Sailing the Sea of Story. Boston, MA: Houghton Mifflin Harcourt, 2015.

Rushdie, Salman. Imaginary Homelands: Essays and Criticism, 1981–1991. London, UK: Granta Books, 1991.

Todorov, Tzvetan. The Poetics of Prose. Ithaca, NY: Cornell University Press, 1977.

Welty, Eudora. The Art of Fiction No. 47. Linda Kuehl. Paris Review. No. 55. (Fall 1972) http://www.theparisreview.org/interviews/4013/the-art-of-fiction-no-47-eudora-welty [accessed 5 April 2017].

Welty, Eudora. The Eye of the Story: Selected Essays and Reviews. New York, NY: Random House, 1978.

Wood, James. How Fiction Works. New York, NY: Farrar, Straus and Giroux, 2008.

Nonfiction

Ellis, Sherry. Now Write! Nonfiction: Memoir, Journalism, and Creative Nonfiction Exercises from Today's Best Writers and Teachers. New York, NY: Jeremy P. Tarcher/Penguin, 2009.

Gornick, Vivian. The Situation and the Story: The Art of Personal Narrative. New York, NY: Farrar, Straus and Giroux, 2001.

Gutkind, Lee. You Can't Make This Stuff Up: The Complete Guide to Writing Creative Nonfiction—From Memoir to Literary Journalism and Everything in Between. Boston, MA: Da Capo Press/Lifelong Books, 2012.

Karr, Mary. The Art of Memoir. New York, NY: HarperCollins, 2015.

Lopate, Phillip. The Art of the Personal Essay: An Anthology from the Classical Era to the Present. New York, NY: Anchor Books, 1994.

Miller, Brenda, and Suzanne Paola. Tell It Slant: Creating, Refining, and Publishing Creative Nonfiction. New York, NY: McGraw-Hill, 2012.

Moore, Dinty W. The Truth of the Matter: Art and Craft in Creative Nonfiction. New York, NY: Pearson/Longman, 2007.

Moore, Dinty W. The Rose Metal Press Field Guide to Writing Flash Nonfiction: Advice and Essential Exercises from Respected Writers, Editors, and Teachers. Brookline, MA: Rose Metal Press, 2012.

Moore, Mary Carroll. Your Book Starts Here: Create, Craft, and Sell Your First Novel, Memoir, or Nonfiction Book. Wilton, NH: Riverbed Press, 2011.

Root, Robert L. The Nonfictionist's Guide: On Reading and Writing Creative Nonfiction. Lanham, MD: Rowman & Littlefield, 2008.

Singer, Margot, and Nicole Walker. Bending Genre: Essays on Creative Nonfiction. New York, NY: Bloomsbury Academic, 2013.

Zinsser, William. On Writing Well: The Classic Guide to Writing Nonfiction. New York, NY: HarperCollins, 2006.

Playwriting

Alterman, Glenn. Writing the 10-Minute Play: A Book for Playwrights and Actors Who Want to Write Plays. Milwaukee, WI: Hal Leonard Corporation, 2013.

Ball, David. Backwards and Forwards: A Technical Manual for Reading Plays. Carbondale, IL: Southern Illinois University Press, 1983.

Cole, Toby. Playwrights on Playwriting: The Meaning and Making of Modern Drama from Ibsen to Ionesco. New York, NY: Hill and Wang, 1960.

Downs, William Missouri, and Robin U. Russin. Naked Playwriting: The Art, the Craft, and the Life Laid Bare. Los Angeles, CA: Silman-James Press, 2004.

Dunne, Will. The Dramatic Writer's Companion: Tools to Develop Characters, Cause Scenes, and Build Stories. Chicago, IL: The University of Chicago Press, 2009.

George, Kathleen. Playwriting: The First Workshop. Boston, MA: Focal Press, 1994.

Hatcher, Jeffrey. The Art & Craft of Playwriting. Cincinnati, OH: Story Press, 1996.

Neipris, Janet. To Be a Playwright. New York, NY: Routledge, 2005.

Spencer, Stuart. The Playwright's Guidebook. New York, NY: Faber and Faber, Inc., 2002.

Poetry

Addonizio, Kim. Ordinary Genius: A Guide for the Poet Within. New York, NY: W. W. Norton, 2009.

Addonizio, Kim, and Dorianne Laux. The Poet's Companion: A Guide to the Pleasures of Writing Poetry. New York, NY: W. W. Norton, 1997.

Biddinger, Mary, and John Gallaher. The Monkey and the Wrench: Essays into Contemporary Poetics. Akron, OH: University of Akron Press, 2011.

Boland, Eavan. A Journey with Two Maps: Becoming a Woman Poet. New York, NY: W. W. Norton, 2011.

Brown, Deborah, Annie Finch, and Maxine Kumin. Lofty Dogmas: Poets on Poetics. Fayetteville, AR: University of Arkansas Press, 2005.

Friebert, Stuart, David Walker, and David Young. A Field Guide to Contemporary Poetry & Poetics. Oberlin, OH: Oberlin College Press, 1997.

Fussell, Paul. Poetic Meter, and Poetic Form. New York, NY: Random House, 1965.

Hall, Donald. Claims for Poetry. Ann Arbor, MI: University of Michigan Press, 1982.

Hollander, John. Rhyme's Reason: A Guide to English Verse. New Haven, CT: Yale University Press, 1981.

Jakobson, Roman. Six Lectures on Sound and Meaning. Cambridge, MA: MIT Press, 1978.

Oliver, Mary. A Poetry Handbook. San Diego, CA: Harcourt Brace & Co, 1994.

Pound, Ezra. ABC of Reading. New York, NY: New Directions, 1960.

Strand, Mark, and Eavan Boland. The Making of a Poem: A Norton Anthology of Poetic Forms. New York, NY: W. W. Norton, 2000.

Wright, C. D. Cooling Time: An American Poetry Vigil. Port Townsend, WA: Copper Canyon, 2005.

Glossary

Accentual language A language that uses the relative stress of syllables for rhythm or meter.

Active vocabulary All the words you are able to recall and use on a regular basis.

Allegory A systematic use of images or characters to represent ideas or people that usually aren't named in a text.

Alliteration Repetition of the initial sound of words in a sequence.

Ambiguity The quality of having more than one interpretation or meaning.

Analogy An extended, detailed comparison between two things.

Anaphora The repetition of the same word or phrase at the beginning of a series of sentences, stanzas, lines, or phrases, often with some variation in a long series.

Antagonist The character who works against the interests of the protagonist.

Aside A theatrical convention where dialogue is spoken to the audience, not to the other characters.

Assonance The repetition of vowel sounds across a passage where the vowel sounds can appear in any position of the words.

Authorial voice The role of the writer in a work of fiction or nonfiction; this is not always the same as the narrator's voice.

Automatic writing The surrealist technique of writing whatever words come to mind without conscious, ethical, or esthetic control.

Backstory Information about the narrative past that is included in narration but not portrayed as a scene or half-scene.

Beat A point in a scene when the character's motivation or objective changes. Or in stage directions within dialogue, a beat can indicate a pause.

Blocking Directions, usually given by the director of a play, to tell the actors where to stand and what to do.

Cadavre exquis A surrealist technique involving a group of writers who each write parts of a sentence without knowing what the other has written (the name means exquisite corpse).

Caesura A pause in the middle of a line of poetry, which may come at the halfway point or approximately one-third or two-thirds of the way through the line.

Cast of characters A listing of the characters in a play, often with a brief description of each.

Central narration When the narrator of a story is a character that is central to the action of the story.

Character sketch A description of the character's appearance, possessions, history, and relationships that a writer may draw on to understand the character's motivations.

Cinematic narration The choice to limit the narrator of a story to describe only the external images, actions, and dialogue of the characters.

Cliché An overused phrase.

Code switching The ability to change diction, accent, and vocabulary based on the context.

Collage A nonlinear strategy for revision, where you cut up what you have written and rearrange it to find new patterns and possibilities.

Concrete poetry Poetry where the visual arrangement of the words on the page is as or more important than the sounds of the words.

Connotation Other meanings that are associated with a word.

Consonance The repetition of consonant sounds across a passage where the consonants can appear in any position of the words.

Dada A precursor to surrealism that sought to explore nonsense through random combinations of words, sound poems, and collage, in order to challenge the existing cultural order.

Déjà vu The sensation of having been somewhere or experienced something before when that isn't true.

Denotation The primary meaning of a word.

Depth The choice in narration of whether to reveal thoughts and feelings of a character, and how much to reveal.

Dialect Regional speech.

Dialogue The recorded speech of characters in a story or play, usually indicated by putting the words within quotation marks and including some form of attribution.

Diction The combination of word choice and word order.

Dramatic irony When actions or dialogue in a previous scene contradict the characters in the present scene, while some or all of the characters on stage are unaware of the previous scene.

Dramatic monologue A poem that recounts a character's speech as if it were said in a specific context, usually to another character.

Ekphrasis Poetry or other writing about a work of art, primarily visual art, though other art forms may be included.

End rhyme Rhyme that occurs in the final syllables of a line in poetry.

Enjambment Placing a line break at a point in the sentence where there is not a natural pause.

Epilogue A scene at the end of a story or novel that takes place well after the main concluding events of the story.

Epistolary novel A novel or story told through the exchange of letters, usually with two or more narrators.

Epistrophe The repetition of the same word or phrase at the end of a series of sentences, stanzas, lines, or phrases, often with some variation in a long series.

Exposition Dialogue describing an event that has previously occurred off-stage.

Extended metaphor A detailed description of one thing in terms of another.

Fable The chronological sequence of all events that make up the story.

Flash-forward A scene or half-scene that takes place after the concluding scene of the story, in the narrative future.

Flashback A scene or half-scene that takes place before the first scene of a story, in the narrative past.

Flat characters Usually minor characters that are not fully developed.

Foreshadowing The introduction of an action, prop, or information in dialogue that gives a hint of what will happen in the future.

Forward-story Information about the narrative future that is included in narration but not portrayed as a scene or half-scene.

Found poem A poem made out of an existing text by breaking it into lines in order to highlight certain elements or to bring out a hidden meaning.

Free verse Poetry that does not use traditional verse forms, but instead invents a new form for each poem.

Genre A form or type of writing such as poetry, fiction, nonfiction, or drama; or a sub-type of the form, such as genres of fiction: romance, science fiction, fantasy, detective fiction, thriller, etc.

Half-scene A moment of scenic development in a story that does not develop a full sense of conflict or resolution.

Idiom A common phrase or figure of speech.

Image The representation of a perception or thing; though often visual, images can also include the other senses.

Immediate narration When the narrator tells a story as it is happening or just after it has happened with no time for reflection.

Inciting incident An event that has already occurred at the start of a play and that precipitates the action of the play.

Internal rhyme Rhyme that occurs within a line or lines of poetry, but not at the end of the line.

Irony To say one thing but mean the opposite; in fiction, when the characters or narrator express views that the author implies are contradicted by other evidence in the story.

Journey A story pattern where characters move from one place to another, usually with a goal in mind and with some complications along the way.

Juxtaposition Placing words or images in close proximity to one another, often used in poetry.

Kenning An Anglo-Saxon poetic device of naming something by combining two words that describe it.

Limited narration A third person narrator who reveals only the actions and thoughts of one focal character in the story.

List poem A poem, often in free verse, that takes its form from a list, and makes use of anaphora, epistrophe, and other forms of repetition with variation.

Metaphor In general, the comparison between two things that are mostly different; specifically, the identification of two things, often using "is."

Metonymy The comparison of two related things, such as using a related image to name something.

Motivation The desires, goals, and inner conflicts that drive a character to action.

Narration The passages of a story between scenes when the narrator summarizes what happens over a period of time.

Narrative arc A model of the conflict, rising tensions, crisis, and resolution of a story.

Narrative break An extra line of space between paragraphs, often marked with "###," that indicates a shift in time or perspective.

Narrative future Everything that will take place after the concluding scene of the story.

Narrative past Everything that has happened before the first scene of the story.

Narrative present The main chronology of a story; the present time that takes place between the first and the last scenes.

Narrator The voice that tells a story; sometimes the author and sometimes a distinct character.

Negative capability The ability, especially in poetry, to present opposite images or emotions without resolving their contradictions.

Off rhyme Rhyme where the vowel sound is somewhat different, also called slant rhyme: "weak" and "bake" might be considered off rhymes.

Omniscient narration A third person narrator who is able to reveal all the actions and all the thoughts of all the characters in a story.

Outline A linear strategy for revision, where you map out all the elements of the piece you are writing.

Oxymoron A phrase that appears to be made up of words with opposite qualities.

Paradox An image or character that combines contradictory elements.

Passive vocabulary All the words you recognize when you read or hear them.

Perfect rhyme see *True rhyme*.

Persona The outward character or a role someone takes on.

Persona poem A poem written in the voice of a character, not the author.

Personification Portraying animals or inanimate objects or forces with human qualities.

Plot The order in which the events of a story are revealed to the reader, which may be chronological or not. In general terms, the plot also refers to the action of the story; in specific terms (especially in contrast to the fable), it refers to the way the action is patterned in the story.

Poetic license The freedom in poetry and other forms of creative writing to change the truth for artistic reasons.

Point of attack The moment when the central conflict of a play is introduced through action or dialogue.

Point of view The perspective from which a story is told; the person speaking as the narrator and how much that person knows.

Prose poem A poem that is written in one or more paragraphs instead of in lines; it uses poetic language and imagery, but does not use the line to organize them.

Protagonist The main character, usually someone the audience or reader sympathizes with.

Pun A play on similar-sounding words that have different meanings or wordplay with different meanings of one word.

Quantitative language A language that uses the relative duration of syllables for rhythm or meter.

Quest A story pattern where the characters go in search of something and return after finding it or failing in their quest.

Question and answer poem A poem, often in free verse, that alternates questions and answers or lists a series of questions followed by a list of their answers, which often are indirect or oblique.

Recognized forms Definitions, job applications, letters, personal ads, and other common texts can be used as models for the structure of a poem.

Reflective narration When the narrator tells a story some time after it has happened and has had time for reflection.

Removed narration When the narrator tells a story long after it has happened and knows other perspectives but may have forgotten or misremembered some of the details.

Rhyme Words with similar sounds; usually the same final sounds in the last stressed and unstressed syllables.

Rhyme scheme The regular pattern of end rhyme across a stanza or stanzas of a poem.

Rule of threes The principle that important elements of a plot ought to appear three times, first introduced, then reinforced, then actually used.

Scene A unit in fiction or nonfiction where the characters and actions are portrayed in detail and time seems to be slowed down; also a unit of drama where one sequence of events is portrayed, usually in one place and for a limited period of time.

Simile A comparison of two things, often using "like" or "as."

Slant rhyme See *Off rhyme*; some differentiate off rhyme and slant rhyme by degree where the vowel sounds in slant rhyme are usually closer to true rhyme than in off rhyme.

Soliloquy A theatrical convention where a character says his or her inner thoughts out loud.

Speaker of the poem The implied character whose voice is portrayed in a poem.

Stage directions The directions about the scene, characters, and actions that the playwright includes in the script for the director and actors.

Stage lie Dialogue in a play that is contradicted by the actions of the character speaking. Usually only the audience can see the action.

Stereotype A character that is based on a familiar type.

Stream of consciousness When the narrative voice reveals only what the narrator perceives and is thinking over the course of a story as it happens.

Subtext The unspoken messages we interpret by reading between the lines of dialogue.

Surrealism A literary and artistic movement that attempted to discover a heightened reality by exploring the dream and the subconscious mind, writing without conscious, esthetic, or moral control.

Symbol An image that represents something else, often an abstract concept which isn't named in the text.

Synecdoche A form of metonymy that uses a part to refer to the whole.

Synesthesia To describe one sense perception in terms of another.

Syntax The order of words in a sentence and the grammatical rules that determine and help decode word order.

Telescoping The combination of elements that occurred over a period of time in one scene or in a shorter span of time.

Thesaurus A reference book of synonyms, antonyms, and related words. There are dictionary-style thesauruses that list a few words and conceptual thesauruses that list many more words around related concepts.

Thought The internal monologue of a character. Some narrators reveal this to the reader.

True rhyme When the final sounds of two words are identical, though the initial sound of the final syllable is different: "pot" and "hot".

Unreliable narrator A narrator who is misinformed or who presents misinformation that the details of the story contradict.

Visitation A story pattern where the action starts when a new character enters the setting and ends when the character leaves.

Voice The way a character, narrator, or speaker of a poem speaks, created through the choice of words and diction.

Voiceover Dialogue in a play that is spoken by an actor off stage or recorded dialogue played through the sound system.

Volta A rhetorical turn, typically found in a sonnet after the octet.

Well-rounded character A character portrayed as multifaceted, complex, and even contradictory.

Witness narration When the narrator of a story is a character that is peripheral to the action of the story and only witnesses it.

Writer's block The feeling that you can't write because you haven't written anything already; a vicious cycle that your instructor can help you overcome.

Zero draft An imperfect and partially developed initial draft the intention of which is to explore an idea to its end point.

Index

CPSIA information can be obtained
at www.ICGtesting.com
Printed in the USA
LVHW03s0957150818
586963LV00022B/564/P